Buried Treasure

By Lloyd and Jennifer Laing in Piccolo
The Young Archaeologist's Handbook

Jennifer Laing
Buried Treasure

Text illustrations by Hetty Baillie-Grohman and Jane Cope
Cover photograph by Rayment Kirby

Piccolo Original Pan Books

First published 1978 by Pan Books Ltd,
Cavaye Place, London SW10 9PG
© Jennifer Laing 1978
ISBN 0 330 25438 3
Printed and bound in Great Britain by
Cox & Wyman Ltd, London, Reading and Fakenham

Contents

2 Treasure hunts

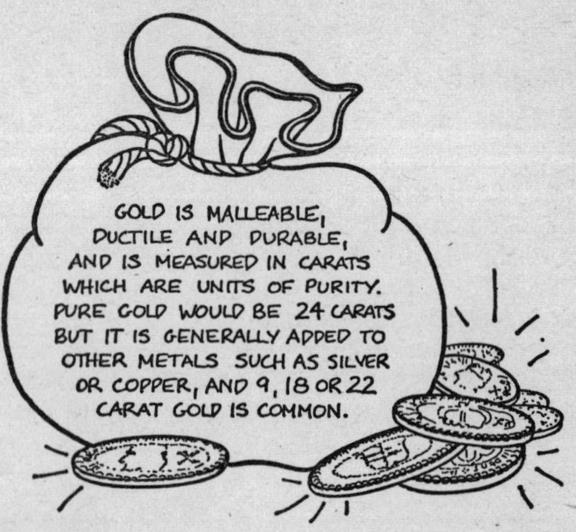

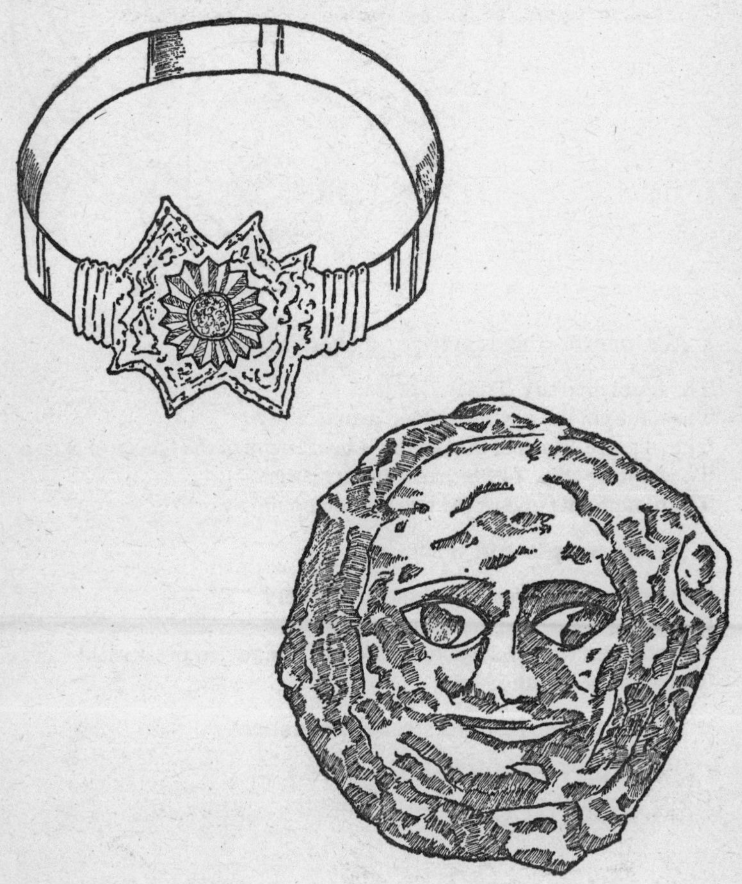

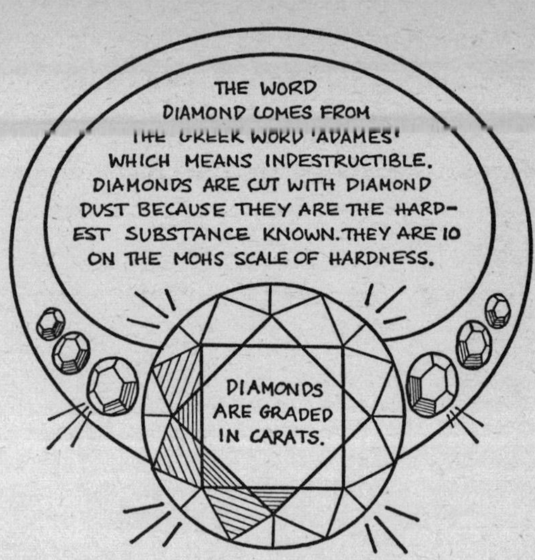

5 Accidental discoveries and excavations

The sea of mercury The wall of iron
The tombs of the Scythian blood drinkers
The treasure tombs of the Scyths The treasure of the Queen of Sumer
The treasure ship The lavender field treasure
The plough that uncovered two million pounds-worth of treasure

6 Young people and treasure

The treasures of Priam The golden jewellery
Golden cuttlefish and golden masks
The children who broke pots for sweets The golden potato field
The porpoise and the stone

7 Pirate treasures and sunken treasures

Captain Kidd's treasure The treasure trick
Henry Morgan's treasure Sunken treasures

8 How to find treasure

Safety first Ancient sites Permission Do not leave a mess
Reporting finds The country code Keeping records Where to search
How to know when you have found treasure
Common treasures you might find Aids to treasure hunting

DATE	TREASURE	LOCATION
3:3:78	Twisted metal about 3 feet long. Silver?	In Eastern corner of field next to Post Office in village of Snodbury. Sticking out of furrow.
9:3:78	Crock of gold coins	Corner of filled-in building site at Grange street, Birmingpool. Lying on the ground at the end of a rainbow.

Introduction

If you go to the seaside you will be able to paddle or swim your way through billions of tons of gold. You will touch some of it, you may even swallow some, but you will not be able to see it, because the sea contains huge amounts of gold, but in such a tiny proportion that it is too expensive to extract. Anyone wanting to find treasure could do worse than invent a cheap method of taking gold from the sea.

The traditional method of finding treasure is to dig at the end of the rainbow. Unfortunately the end of the rainbow always moves further away as we move towards it. The same thing happens with many treasures.

Nevertheless, as soon as the fever for treasure hits people they will go to crazy lengths to find it: people have killed, tortured and maimed, defied curses and risked their lives to find treasure. Some of the real-life adventures of treasure hunters sound like fairy tales.

Most of the things we think of as treasure – gold, silver, diamonds, rubies or emeralds – have important uses as well as beauty. Some people have believed that precious stones have special magical powers, and we keep up this belief today when we wear birthstones. Treasures of nearly every kind spend most of their time buried – under the sea, underground, in bank vaults or strongrooms. It is for this reason alone that they are difficult to mine in the first place, or to steal later. Unfortunately the lure of treasure inspires many crooks to great efforts, and some of the most exciting treasure hunts have been illegal.

Finding treasure

The most interesting and exciting thing about treasure is finding it yourself. Everyone would like to find treasure, even if they are already happy or do not want to be very rich. It is surprising how many people have actually found treasures of great value and interest. In fact, more people are finding splendid treasures nowadays than ever before, so your chances of finding some of your own are very high. In the past the people who found treasures most often were farmers ploughing fields and men building roads or houses. Because they were not looking for treasure and were used to upturning useless bits of metal, they often did not recognize the treasures they had found, but thought them rubbish. Nowadays, however, there are many books to help treasure hunters recognize the things they find, and many museums where you can see treasures displayed. By studying treasures that have already been found you can learn to recognize treasure when you find it. Treasures rarely come out of the ground or the dust of attics looking new and shiny, so even the muddiest, dirtiest object you might find has a chance of being valuable and exciting.

Many treasures are not buried in the ground at all, and no digging is needed to find them. Sometimes people have found treasures in their own attics or cellars. It is worth looking through cupboards and garden sheds too – a good spring clean can pay handsomely. Never throw anything away before making sure that it really is rubbish! The old china pot that your grandmother used might be worth a fortune, or the piece of brass an uncle brought back from sea could be a collector's piece now. It is also possible to find treasures of one sort or another in junk shops or market stalls, but

you would have to pay some money for them, so it is probably not worth while taking the chance until you are really sure what is treasure and what is not.

In order not to miss any treasure you might find – whether in an attic or in the ground – you would have to be an expert in many different subjects. It is probably best to start looking first, see what you find, and then have fun discovering whether it is valuable or not. You may be surprised what you come up with! The ways you can learn to recognize treasures and how to find them are described in detail in Chapter 8.

In the past the finding of treasures has often been very dangerous. Nowadays there is no need to get into danger or difficulties as long as you stick to the simple rules of treasure hunting (also listed in Chapter 8).

Anyone can find treasure if they are observant. It does not take special skill, and it need not be hard work. It will certainly be fun. There are so many different types of treasures that there is almost no excuse for not finding *something* of value!

Remember that you should never throw anything away without asking yourself if it could be valuable. If the answer is 'yes', make sure about it by reading library books, asking experts or combing museums.

The most difficult part of treasure hunting is knowing when you have found a fortune. It is therefore a good idea to know what some common treasures look like and what they might be used for. If you find a piece of yellowish metal that is covered in rust, for instance, you should know immediately that it cannot be gold since this metal does not rust. The following pages will give you an idea why some objects are regarded as treasures and what makes them special.

It can also be helpful to know about some of the greatest treasure hunts. You can learn from the hunters' failures or successes. Some treasure hunts have been incredible adventures and you can read about them in this book.

1 The facts

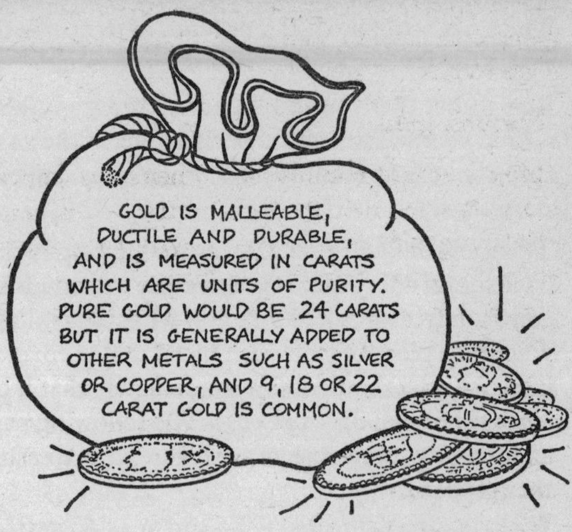

Gold

Gold, a heavy yellow metallic element, is very difficult to destroy and is therefore highly prized. It is resistant to acids and is not affected by changes in temperature, but it can be melted down into almost any shape. It is for this reason that gold has been popular with thieves, who have been able to get rid of stolen gold items, without losing their value, simply by lighting a fire. Sovereigns, crowns, buckles, jewellery, cups, statues and wine jugs made of gold have all found their way into the melting-pot at some time. It is amazing to think that the gold we see in jewellers' shop windows could well contain some melted down treasure that once belonged to famous or infamous people – Henry VIII of England, Julius Caesar, or Mary Queen of Scots; Attila the Hun, or Ivan the Terrible.

The golden chamber pot

When, on 27 April 1966, the British government declared a limit to the number of gold sovereigns that any one person could hoard, one enterprising man had his coins melted down and recast into the shape of a shining but costly chamber pot. Unfortunately for him, the government reversed its order a few years later to allow people to own as many as they could afford to buy. The value of the golden potty was then much lower than it would have been in sovereigns. Someone else with a golden sense of humour had a solid gold lavatory seat made – but it was padlocked to the bathroom!

Finding gold

Most gold is almost invisible when in its natural state in the ground. It is often found in the form of dust or very small particles. Prospectors have to pan for it in rivers, as the gold is worn away from the rocks around it, and is carried downstream by the water. Since it is about seven times as heavy as the rocks, it sinks to the bottom of the pan when washed in water.

Many prospectors have been misled into wild joy by *iron pyrites*. This mineral is often found in the same areas as gold and it glitters and glints in the sun as though it were the real thing. It is therefore known as *fool's gold*. There is much truth in the old saying, 'All that glitters is not gold.'

Other prospectors have been luckier. During the Australian gold rush (1857–60) large pieces of gold called 'boulders' were found, and some nuggets were so large that they were given names. The largest ever found was the *Holterman* nugget which weighed over 200 pounds (90·72 kg). The *Welcome Stranger* nugget was over 125 pounds (56·7 kg) and the *Sierra Sands* nugget was 93 pounds (42·18 kg).

Gold has been panned for over 5,000 years and some people, particularly the Romans, invented machinery to mine it. Nowadays gold is usually extracted by machinery rather than by hand. The total world production is about 52,000,000 fine ounces each year.

Uses of gold

Gold is widely used for making *jewellery* and beautiful objects. Objects made of gold have often survived for thousands of years when more ordinary objects have long since perished.

The golden astronauts

Gold is a good conductor of electricity and is used in *electrical contacts*. It also reflects about 98 per cent of infra-red radiation. It is therefore important in *space exploration*. The US satellites *Discoverer 14* and the Ranger and Mariner series were protected by gold.

The thickness needed to keep the temperatures comfortable as the satellites sped nearer the sun was only 0·000025 to 0·000005 inches (0·0000635–0·0000127 cm).

Astronaut Edward H. White had a helmet to rival the golden helmets of ancient warriors when he was projected into space in *Gemini 4*. His visor was plated with gold to filter out the infra-red and ultraviolet radiation.

Gold in medicine

Gold has been used in *dental surgery* for many years because it does not rust and is not affected by eating hot or cold foods.

Radioactive colloidal gold is used to treat arthritis and is used for some nerve-end operations. A traditional treatment for a stye in the eye is to rub the infected part with a wedding ring.

Gold beating – making a little go a long way

Only minute quantities of gold are needed to cover enormous areas, because gold can be beaten so thin that it becomes translucent. The method of beating gold to make gold leaf (which is used for decorating such luxury items as leather-bound books) has been known since the time of the Ancient Greeks. The Greek writer Homer tells how a hammer and anvil was used in gold beating. It is doubtful if the Ancient Greeks were able to carry out the intricate beating that is possible today, however.

To make gold leaf, the gold is first added to a small quantity of silver or copper to make it workable. An ingot 2 in (5·08 cm) long, $1\frac{1}{8}$ in (2·85 cm) wide and $\frac{1}{8}$ in (0·32 cm) thick is run between two electrically operated rollers to produce a thin strip 20 ft (6 m) long, $1\frac{1}{8}$ in (2·85 cm) wide and a mere $\frac{1}{1000}$ in (0·00254 cm) thick. This is then cut into 200 squares each one $1\frac{1}{8}$ by $1\frac{1}{8}$ in (2·85 by 2·85 cm). It is then ready for the first beating process. The gold square is placed carefully in a *cutch* or packet of heavy paper or vellum. It is then enclosed in sheepskin to protect it from the hammer, and beaten until it is 4 in (10·16 cm) square. Because it is so fragile at this stage, it is handled with wooden tongs and placed on a cushion where it is cut into four. The 2-in (5·08 cm) squares are then placed between skins (made from the intestines of cattle) and beaten until they are 4 in (10·16 cm) square again. By this time the gold is so fragile that it cannot be cut with steel. Instead it is cut in four with a *wagon* – a kind of small sled with Malacca reed runners.

Each square is then placed on a mould of about 5 in (12·7 cm)
square and beaten until the mould is covered. The gold is then
placed on a leather cushion. At this stage it is so fragile that it can
be straightened on the cushion with a mere puff of breath! The
gold is then ready for use in gilding and ornamentation and is
stored in books of 25 leaves each.

How to make gold

If I knew how to do this, I should probably not be writing this
book, but many people in the past have tried to make gold. The
alchemists in the Middle Ages spent nearly all their time trying to
produce the valuable metal from iron or lead. So far as we know
they were not successful, but modern chemistry grew up as a side-
effect of their researches. Even though they did not find gold they
found a 'treasure-store' of knowledge. As it happens, we cannot be
absolutely certain that they did not find a way to make gold – there
is even a rumour that the Bank of England was founded on gold
made in an alchemist's laboratory. If gold was made, it is possible
that the knowledge would have been kept secret deliberately. We
shall probably never know.

The king who prized iron more than gold

Gold is much easier to work than iron and for this reason it was
widely used long before the secret of making iron objects from iron
ore was discovered. The Egyptians had plenty of gold and made it
into beautiful and useful objects, but they did not know how to work
iron until late in their history. The only people who did know were
the Egyptians' rivals – the Hittites. They lived in what is now
Turkey and they guarded their secret for centuries, although
many attempts were made to find out. Brave men probably went to
spy in the Hittite kingdom. If they discovered the secret, they did
not live to tell the tale. The young king Tutankhamun of Egypt
(see p. 47) was buried with a great many treasures of gold. But under
his head was an iron headrest, and nearby in the tomb were two iron
daggers – obviously prized more highly than the gold! He must
have been given them, or have bought them from the Hittites. It was
not until the Hittites had troubles amongst their rulers and the
empire broke up that the secret of iron-working became known
all over the world. If it were not for this, we might still be using
gold and bronze instead of iron and steel.

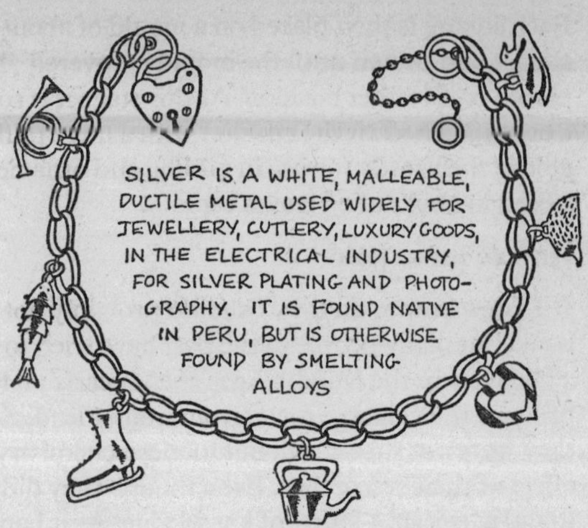

Silver

Silver has been less sought after than gold because it tarnishes very easily, and constant polishing wears it away. All metals were first polished by being rubbed with fine sand, but modern metal polishes are almost as harmful. Silver that has been in the soil for some time can be totally destroyed but gold remains intact. A purple stain in the ground is often all that remains of the most beautiful silver objects. Even so, silver is very valuable.

Uses of silver

Silver is widely used for *cutlery* and *tableware*, though there are few people today who can afford solid silver cups and plates like many rich people in the past. Silver-plated cutlery is more common, but still expensive compared to steel. Silver is the best conductor of electricity, and it is therefore used in *electrical contacts*. Silver compounds, such as bromides and chlorides, darken when exposed to the light, so they are used in *photographic processes. Jewellery* is also made out of silver.

Silver plating

Although many different methods have been used to plate other metals with silver in the past, the method most commonly used today is *electro-plating*. When you see the letters EPNS on a silver object it is Electro-Plated Nickel Silver, which means that it is made with a coating of silver on a core of another metal. The technique was invented as long ago as 1836 by two Englishmen,

George and Henry Elkington. As the name suggests, the process involves passing a current of electricity through a bath in which there is a solution of silver salts. The object to be plated is immersed in the bath and wired to the positive pole of the current, the negative pole being wired to a piece of the plating metal (or something inert like a piece of graphite).

Electrum

This is an alloy of gold and silver that was very common in ancient times. It was sometimes found as a natural alloy in Turkey, and some of the oldest coins in the world were made from it.

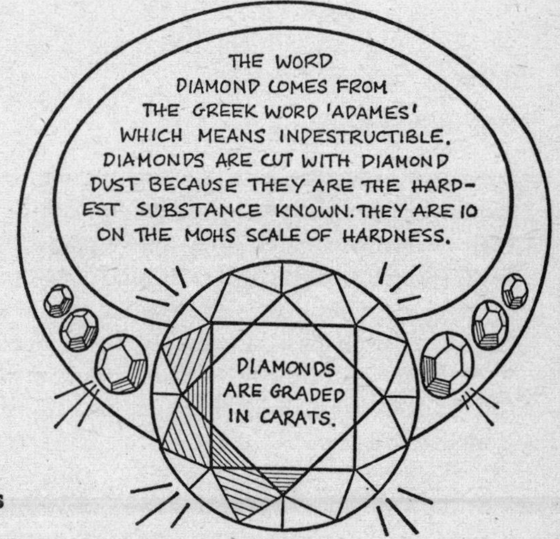

Diamonds are a girl's best friends

Diamonds are formed in the earth – possibly as much as 75 miles below the surface, so they are well and truly *buried treasure*. It takes millions of years to produce one diamond in the heat and pressure below the earth's surface. The diamonds are then pushed towards the surface by volcanic activity in rock known as Kimberlite, after the famous *Kimberley diamond mines* in South Africa. One engagement ring thus takes an incredible number of years to make!

Diamonds are graded in carats; the word comes from carob – an oriental bean which was used for weighing gems because each bean was the same size. In precious stones, one carat weighs 0·200 grams. A one-carat diamond is quarter-inch diameter, but an eight-carat stone is only half-inch diameter. The largest diamond found in Brazil that could be cut into a gem was the *Star of the South*, which weighed 261·3 carats. It was found in 1853.

Diamonds are not all sparkling, clear stones. *Dort* is poorly crystallized diamond, *balas* is hard and used in industry, as is the grey or black *carbonado*. The largest carbonado mass was the *Sergio* diamond from Brazil. It weighed 3,167 carats.

Diamond is the hardest natural substance known, and is pure carbon. When they come out of the ground diamonds are not sparkling gems; they are dull, unattractive and greasy-looking. They were first found over 5,000 years ago in Indian river beds, and the largest stones have come from this area. India traded diamonds as far afield as ancient Rome, Greece and China until the trade was upset in 1725 (see below).

The diamond gambling tallies

In 1725 prospectors were looking for gold in the State of Minas Gerais, Brazil. They were miles from civilization and had to make their own amusements. They were already gambling their lives and fortunes on finding gold, so it is not surprising that their chief pastime was gambling. They fell into the habit of using pebbles from the river beds for the tallies. These were eventually discovered to be diamonds, and many fortunes were made. Many fortunes (particularly of those whose money was tied up with the Indian trade) were lost too. The town of Tejuco was renamed Diamantina.

The small boy who discovered a diamond field

A small boy, playing near the banks of the Orange River in South Africa near Hopetown found an interesting pebble one day. After some time the 'pebble' found its way on to the market and was sold uncut (and therefore less valuable, see p. 26) for £875. It is known as the *Eureka* diamond (this means 'I have found it!') or the *O'Reilly* diamond after the dealer. The rush to the South African diamond fields began soon after. Prospectors who had been unlucky in finding gold hurried to the area and by 1870 over 10,000 men were looking for diamonds using the most primitive methods. Today, as a result of the small boy's find, 95 per cent of the world's diamonds come from South Africa.

The Aga Khan who was weighed in diamonds

In 1946 the Aga Khan, the spiritual leader of the Moslems, weighed 243 pounds (110·20 kg). This fact was of vital importance to his followers. To celebrate his 75th birthday he held a Diamond Jubilee. He said that his followers must give his weight in diamonds to various charities. He sat, an impressive figure, in a brocade-canopied chair as case after case of industrial diamonds were brought to counterbalance him. Finally, nearly half a million industrial diamonds, on loan from the London Diamond Syndicate, were needed before the balance was correct. The cost of these diamonds was estimated to be about $1½ million. The sultans and rajahs and princes then paid their dues in cash.

This is even more astonishing when you think that for every half-carat diamond to reach the shops, over 46,000 pounds (20,865 kg) of rock has been blasted, crushed and collected at the surface of the mines. It has been ground up and then spun in revolving drums with grease at the bottom. The larger diamonds have been removed by eye, but the smaller are attracted to the grease and are collected from the bottom of the drums. Diamond mining is not an easy or a quick job.

Famous diamonds

The largest diamond in the world was the *Cullinan*. When it was found it was the size of a man's fist and was an enormous 3,106 carats. No less than eight of the world's largest diamonds and ninety-six lesser stones were cut from it. It came from the Premier Mine in South Africa, and was named after the president of the mine, Sir Thomas Cullinan. Although the machinery was working deep in the mine, on 25 January 1905, Captain Frederick Wells just happened to see the vast stone lying at the surface near what was known as the Big Hole. It is thought that it was only part of a much larger diamond but the rest was never discovered.

The largest stone cut from the Cullinan is known as the *Star of Africa*. It is pear-shaped, and 2⅛ inches (5·4 cm) long, and 530·20 carats. It is now in the Royal Sceptre of the British Crown Jewels.

Three other stones cut from the Cullinan are also in the British Crown Jewels: the Cullinan II is now in the Imperial Crown, the Cullinan III can be found in the finial of the Queen's crown and the Cullinan IV is set in the Queen's crown too, along with the *Kohinoor*.

The Kohinoor has had a very stormy history and many people disagree over exactly what happened to it. In 1304 it was owned by the Rajah of Malawa, India, and by 1525 it was in the possession of the first Mogul Emperor, Sultan Baber. Later it was owned by the Indian prince who built the Taj Mahal. The Persians invaded India in 1739 under their leader Nadir Shah. They seized the Imperial jewels, but the Kohinoor was not to be found. Searches and questions followed – Delhi was pillaged and burnt – but still the diamond did not turn up.

Finally, one of the harem girls of the deposed Indian leader told Nadir Shah that the Prince kept the diamond in his turban. Nadir Shah then thought up a cunning plot to get the diamond. He set the Prince up in his rightful position once more and worked out a ceremony of goodwill to 'cement the friendship'. During the ceremony he suggested (to the Indian prince's surprise and sorrow) that they should exchange turbans as a sign of their friendship and trust. The Indian ruler could do nothing but agree. He handed over the turban and the Persian rushed back to his apartments to open it up. It is said that when the Nadir Shah saw the stone sparkling among the folds of the turban he exclaimed 'Kohinoor!' which means 'Mountain of Light!'

The adventures of the diamond were not over yet. It seems that the Shah was killed, and his son died under torture rather than reveal where it was hidden. It fell into the hands of Ranjit Singh, the *Lion of the Punjab*. In 1849 a mutiny led to Britain taking over the Punjab, and the Kohinoor was taken into the possession of the East India Company and in the end was presented to Queen Victoria. The queen was not satisfied with the diamond – it did not sparkle as much as she would have liked, so she ordered that it should be recut. After 38 days of hard work the diamond cutters finished the work. The Kohinoor is now in the crown which was worn by Queen Elizabeth II at her coronation in 1953, and is kept in the Tower of London.

The *Regent* is another diamond around which many stories have been woven. One story tells of a slave who ran away and gave the diamond to a sea captain in return for his passage to freedom. With the diamond safely in his possession, the captain threw the slave overboard and then sold the gem to an Indian merchant. The captain is then said to have lived riotously on the proceeds and ended up by hanging himself in remorse. Whatever the truth of the early days of the diamond, it was bought by the Governor of Madras, Sir William Pitt (for this reason it is sometimes known as the Pitt diamond) in 1702. He paid the enormous sum of £35,000 for it. It was later sold to the Regent of France (hence its name). The Regent acted as king until the monarch grew up. It was stolen along with the rest of the French crown jewels in 1792, but was recovered. Later, Napoleon had it mounted into the hilt of his ceremonial sword. In 1940, when Paris was occupied by the Germans, the diamond was successfully hidden until after the war, and it is in the Louvre today.

The *Orloff* diamond was first heard of by Europeans in 1750, when reports came in that an idol in Mysore, India, had two huge diamond eyes. A French grenadier became determined to own these. He pretended to believe in the Hindu faith and managed to get the job of guardian of the idol. His deception allowed him to prise one diamond off the idol and escape. He is supposed to have sold the stone to a sea captain for £3,500. Like the slave in the story of the Regent diamond, the grenadier had no luck with the captain who drugged him and had him thrown overboard. After what were probably many adventures, the diamond was bought by Prince Gregory Orloff in 1774. The prince had been spurned by Queen Catherine the Great of Russia, and he hoped to gain her favour by giving her the diamond. She accepted the gift of this small egg-shaped stone and had it mounted in her Imperial sceptre. It is now in the Kremlin in Moscow.

A diamond which disappeared completely was the *Great Moghul*. This was supposed to have been shaped like an egg cut in half, and was at one point in the palace at Delhi. It was probably taken away by the Nadir Shah at the same time that he tried to find the Kohinoor, and after this it disappeared. Several other diamonds have been thought to be this diamond, but it is more likely that it was broken up and recut into several other stones to avoid the detection of the crime.

A typical get-rich-quick story is attached to the *Jonker* diamond. It is a heartening tale among so many stories of diamonds with violent histories and should be an inspiration to all treasure hunters. The Jonker diamond was found by a prospector in Pretoria called Jacobus Jonker, who had spent most of his 62 years in not very successful prospecting. On 18 January 1934, the day after he found the diamond, he sold it for £110,250!

Other famous diamonds are the *Hope* (see p. 52) which is a rare blue colour (diamonds can be almost any colour), the *Florentine* (a lovely yellow diamond which has now disappeared) and the *Shah*, which had three inscriptions about its owners on it.

Other precious stones

The song with the line, *Open up dem pearly gates* is referring to the idea that the gates of heaven are studded with pearls. The heavenly city is supposed to have jasper walls and to be resting on precious stones.

Gems have often been thought to have mystical powers. The modern birthstone is a left-over from a much more ancient belief that gems will look after the wearer. You may be surprised what terrible fates you could be saved from by wearing your birthstone!

Birthstones

January/Garnet This can be red, orange, pale or deep green, brown, violet, purple or colourless. It used to be known as the carbuncle, and was supposed to be able to make its wearer invisible on certain occasions.

February/Amethyst This is really a form of quartz and can be pale or dark purple. Ancient people thought it would prevent drunkenness. Quartz is used in a variety of ways – the World War II crystal radio sets needed it, and modern accurate watches use quartz.

March/Aquamarine This varies from pale blue to deep blue or bluish-green.

April/Diamond This was reputed to give its wearer strength in battle and to protect him from ghosts and magic. It is commonly used in engagement rings – people hope that the long-lasting diamond will be a symbol of their love.

May/Emerald This is, at best, a deep green. It was once dedicated to Venus, goddess of love, and was believed to be good for the eyesight if a person stared at it long enough. If placed on the tongue the emerald was supposed to give the gift of prophesy. The ancient Peruvians were said to have worshipped an emerald the size of an ostrich egg.

June/Pearl Pearls can be almost any colour from white through pink and blue to black. They are produced by non-edible oysters and freshwater mussels. If a piece of grit finds its way into the shell the mollusc coats it with many layers of mother-of-pearl to make it smooth and stop it irritating. Eventually in this way a pearl is formed. Cultured pearls are made deliberately.

July/Ruby This is a red corundum – blue corundums are sapphires. Ruby is used in laser beams. It traditionally ensures love and serenity. The ancient Greeks thought it could melt wax. It was also thought to be able to warm up the corpses of mummies and to cure bleeding if taken as medicine.

August/Peridot This is olive green and supposedly has many mystical powers. It was once thought to be able to break evil spells and have medicinal powers.

September/Sapphire These stones can vary from pink to blue. The largest sapphire in the world is the *Star of India*, and is 563 carats. Sapphires are traditionally a symbol of heavenly bliss and they protect their owner from poverty, betrayal and eye disease. Sapphire is also supposed to cure snake bites.

October/Opal Until the novel *Anne of Geierstein* was written by Sir Walter Scott in 1829, the opal was popular. The story included an opal which had an evil influence, and sales of opals fell. The opal is a creamy-white or black and is lit up by 'sparks' of coloured lights.

November/Topaz This word means fire. The stone is very hard and can vary from the most usual fine yellow colour to pink, blue and green.

December/Turquoise The ancient Egyptians prized this stone, and pieces have been found that were worn over seven and a half thousand years ago. The blue stone can be carved into intricate shapes as well as set in jewellery. Turquoise is supposed to give protection from accidents caused by falling from horses.

Other gems gave specialized protection – the Hyacinth, for instance, was supposed to protect the wearer from being struck by lightning.

The Pope who ate gems

Pope Clement VII is said to have eaten more than 40,000 ducats' worth of gems before he died. The stones were powdered up, and were expected to cure him of his illness. It is definitely not advisable to try this sort of medicinal cure, even if you are rich enough – Clement may have died *because* he ate so many gems.

The jewels that led to everlasting life

Egyptian scarabs were charms in the shape of beetles worn as emblems of resurrection: they were symbols of everlasting life. Some were made of carnelian and amethyst, with a gold plate on the base on which various inscriptions were cut. The scarab beetle lays its eggs in balls of dung which it rolls along the ground, and Egyptians believed that the god Kepher pushed the ball of the sun over the horizon just as the scarab pushed its dung.

Gem cutting

Many precious stones have far less value when they are found than after they have been cut. The art of cutting facets (faces) which show off the colour of the stone and reflect the light is very skilled. Gems were not facetted to make them sparkle until the French invented a method of doing this in the fifteenth century. Instead they were merely polished, usually with very fine sand and water. For this reason older gems often do not glitter as much as modern stones.

The finest medieval crown is that known as the *Imperial Crown of the Holy Roman Empire*. It was probably made in 961 for the coronation of the Emperor Otto I. It is studded with pearls and polished gems set in gold.

Diamonds are particularly difficult to cut, as they have to be facetted along natural planes. One slip by the cutter and a diamond can be ruined.

Man-made gems

These are not buried treasure at all. Diamonds and emeralds and many other stones can be faked – and nowadays a real man-made

Crown of the Holy Roman Emperors

diamond has been produced. It is still very expensive but is not as hard as the real thing. It does not fool a good jeweller.

Other treasures

Many objects apart from precious stones and metals are often called treasures. They are not the things that make most people's eyes light up, even if they do cost money. People have made fortunes out of selling very dull-sounding things like pottery or wooden panelling. In 1977 saffron was more expensive ounce for ounce than gold (it is a yellow dye obtained from a flower like a crocus which is grown in Turkey). But these things usually have one thing in common: they are easily destroyed. There is no space in this book to describe them, and buried treasure in this book means what it meant to the pirates and tomb robbers of yesteryear.

2 Treasure hunts

The gold rushes

Treasure is most exciting when you find it single-handed. Many fortunes have been made – literally overnight. But many people have lost their health and their livelihoods, even their lives, trying to find treasure. During the gold rushes was the time when the greatest number of people were looking for treasure.

Thousands, smitten with gold fever, rushed first to California, then to Australia, and finally to South Africa and the Klondike. These were rough, wild, lawless days when men staked all on the hope of a few nuggets of gold washed into the streams.

The Californian gold rush and the 'Forty-niners'

In 1848 John Augustus Sutter was having a new sawmill built near the Sacramento river. The contractor found gold, and started one of the most extraordinary events in history. In the following year people from all walks of life flocked to the area; there were preachers and farmers, trappers and miners. Sailors deserted their ships to follow the lure of gold – in San Francisco Bay in July 1850 there were no fewer than 500 deserted ships. People left secure jobs and families and joined the rabble of wanderers and wasters, thieves and criminals, to scrape a fortune in the hills. Over 80,000 men flocked to the foothills in 1849, earning themselves the title *Forty-niners*, and many songs and stories have been made up about them. Law was almost unknown and lynching parties and vigilante committees were as near to justice as the Forty-niners usually came. This was the Wild West at its wildest.

Each man discovered a mere half ounce a day on average, but in one year alone over 2,500,000 ounces reached the dealers.

'Pikes Peak or die'

A second, small gold rush was started about ten years later when a group of Cherokee Indians on their way to California found gold near Denver. Tales went round about the find and prospectors with nothing to lose but their lives rushed to the area in a frenzy, with the motto 'Pikes Peak or die'. Sadly, this motto came true. Starvation and attacks from Indians brought death to many. There was almost no gold to be found, but the native Indian populations became restless because of the hordes of people in their territory. The height of the troubles came when federal troops killed Indians in 1864 at what was known as the Sand Creek massacre.

The Australian gold rush (1857–60)

Australia was in the middle of a depression so the finding of gold
there brought about great changes. As in California, prices and wages
rose to enormous heights as those who struck it rich were able to
pay ridiculous prices for the most common objects. A licence was
necessary to enable the many thousands to prospect or look for gold,
but some were so unlucky that even the price of the licence was too
great for their pockets.

The South African gold rush

A diamond digger called George Harrison started the unlucky
prospectors from other areas rushing to South Africa. In 1886 he
was having no luck finding diamonds, but he did find gold. He sold
his claim for a mere £10, and was never heard of again. It would not
be surprising if he died of heartbreak, for in the following year the
area around what was then the small village of Johannesburg was
declared a gold field. Now there are seven productive fields, which
are worked by expensive machinery. The Kimberley diamond mines
of South Africa were the first to exploit these gold fields because
they already had the heavy equipment and finance necessary.

The Klondike and Bonanza Creek

The Klondike is an area of the Yukon in north-west Canada
bordering on Alaska, and it became the scene of the last great
gold rush. It is an inhospitable land and great hardships were
endured in order to find gold. In an area called Bonanza Creek in
1896 the gravel of the Yukon river and the creeks nearby were found
to be rich in gold. Within three or four years the population of
Dawson had grown to 30,000. All the people had one aim in mind
– to find gold. Four years later came the peak in production when
22 million dollars-worth of gold was produced from the frozen
gravels. By 1910 the men had left, Dawson was a mere ghost of the
town it had once been, and the gold was used up.

The methods of extracting the gold from the frozen wastes had to
be changed from the easy panning methods used in California. In
the north, the ground was frozen so fires had to be lit to thaw it
out, and then steam was used to keep the temperatures up.

The Scottish gold rush

Much less spectacular than the great gold rushes, but nevertheless important to those who took part, was the discovery of gold in Scotland in 1868. John Gilchrist had been hit by gold fever during the Australian gold rush and then turned his attention to the Kildonan Burn in Sutherland, starting a minor rush. Licences were obtained, prospectors arrived and over £12,000-worth of gold was extracted before the supply was finished up. It is probable that a much larger quantity was discovered and sold quietly on the side.

Golden stalactites in the Welsh gold rush

The Romans had worked the mines in Dolaucothi in South Wales after 75 AD, and Welsh gold attracted attention again when disappointed prospectors from the Australian and American gold rushes moved in. The supplies are almost exhausted now, but some of the lodes were said to have had gold 'hanging like stalactites'.

The treasures of Byzantium

It was a young prince, Alexis, who started one of the greatest and most terrible hunts for treasure ever seen. His father was Emperor of Byzantium when the Crusaders were setting out in 1202 to try to regain the Holy Land for the Christians. Unfortunately the Crusaders ran out of money before they reached the Holy Land. They became tired and dispirited since they were living rough and they had seen no loot or fighting.

It was at this point that Prince Alexis arrived and gave them hope of gold. He told them that his father, the Emperor, had been put in prison and his place taken by someone else. If the Crusaders would sail to Byzantium, their show of strength would give the Prince's followers heart to rise up and put him on the throne. In return the Prince would give the Crusaders a fabulous sum of gold, and more troops for their wars.

The Crusaders set sail and arrived at the splendid city with all its riches. Sadly for Alexis, his followers were not as keen on having him as their Emperor as he had thought. At first they would not have him back. In the end he and his father were given the throne to share, but the people would not pay the Crusaders. While Alexis and the people argued about who should pay the knights and princes, another man, Murzuphle, took matters into his own hands.

He had Alexis and his father killed and set himself up as Emperor.
He decided not to give the Crusaders the gold they had been
promised. The Crusaders were left with nothing to do but fight.
They beseiged Byzantium for months until, against all odds, they
broke into the city. The Emperor Murzuphle fled with as much
gold and treasure as he could carry.

As soon as the victors went into the city the Christian spirit left
them. They tore the gold off statues and chiselled it out of columns.
They smashed chandeliers to rip out the silver and tore the jewels
out of inlaid furniture. They took crosses and chalices from churches,
and opened tombs to steal from the dead. They took horses and
carts into the church of St Sophia to take away their loot more
easily. They opened up the tomb of the great Emperor Justinian,
gazed on his corpse which had been preserved for centuries, then
they ripped out all the treasures buried with him. The Crusaders
pulled bronze doors off their hinges and smashed the altar in St
Sophia to seize the rubies and diamonds that adorned it. They took
away all the sacred relics, including no less than ten 'genuine' heads
of St John the Baptist! It was one of the worst acts of vandalism the
world has ever seen, and entirely due to the lust for treasure.
Statues were smashed and people were maimed or killed. At the end
of a week there was an eclipse of the sun. At last the Crusaders were
afraid. Suddenly they remembered their Christian beliefs and the
violence stopped. For the Crusaders the city had been a treasure
trove, but for their victims there was nothing but violence and
horror. The Crusaders never did reach the Holy Land.

The treasure of Montezuma

This is one of the most famous true stories about a great treasure,
but it was much more horrible than the events at Byzantium. The
man who found the treasure was Hernandes Cortes. On 16 August
1519 he set out with a fleet of warships, 110 sailors, 553 soldiers,
10 cannon, 4 light field guns and 16 horses. Against the wishes of the
Governor of Cuba, General Velasquez, he was intent on the conquest
of Mexico.

At this time Mexico was a vast empire ruled over by the Emperor
Montezuma of the Aztecs. Some of the Mexican tribes were not
happy under Montezuma's rule and one tribe helped Cortes and his
Spanish followers. Another advantage that Cortes had was that the

Mexicans had never seen a horse before. They thought that the horse and rider was one animal, and they were terrified. A third advantage was that the Aztecs worshipped a god called Quetzalcoatl whose skin was fair. It is possible that Montezuma thought that Cortes was the god returning.

The goodbye gift of gold

The two sides sent each other messages and Cortes won a number of battles. In the end, Montezuma sent a fabulous 'Goodbye' gift to Cortes, in the hope that he would take the treasures and go. He sent him a huge gold disc that looked like the sun, and another in silver that represented the moon, He gave him 20 golden ducks, and ornaments of gold in the shape of dogs, pumas and monkeys. There were 10 gold necklaces and a golden bow with 12 arrows, 2 golden rods and silver and gold crests with plumes of green feathers. There were fans and models of deer, and 30 bales of cotton material dyed with patterns of many-coloured feathers. It was a fabulous present, but instead of sending the Spaniards away, it merely made them greedy for more.

The Spaniards began moving forward through Aztec lands, but every village they came to was empty. In some of the huts were the horrible remains of the sacrifices carried out by the fleeing people. The Aztecs used to tear out the heart of the human sacrifice while it was still beating. The torn-out hearts and severed legs and arms of the victims were still in the blood-spattered huts. Cortes and his men were disgusted by the rituals, but they were not too squeamish to cut off the hands of fifty of their Mexican friends who were spying for Montezuma!

On 10 November 1519 the Spaniards reached the Aztec capital, a vast city built on an island and surrounded by canals with bridges over them.

Montezuma and Cortes

Montezuma came out to greet the newcomers. He was tall and thin and wore a cape with pearls and precious stones on it. His feet were shod with golden sandals with gold-encrusted straps. He was carried through the streets in a golden paladin. Montezuma was probably not sure if Cortes was a god or not. So he gave the Spaniards a palace to live in and allowed them to put up an altar to their own Christian God.

The treasure store of the Aztecs

As the Spaniards were preparing a room for their altar, they made their greatest discovery. They noticed an outline of a door in some fresh plaster. Opening it up they found a treasure store of gold, silver, dyed feathers, gorgeous clothes and jewels. It was the treasure of the Aztec emperors, gathered together over many years and buried in the walls.

The problem was how to take it away. It never occurred to them that they had no right to steal the treasure. They blocked up the door again and waited. Their chance came when one of the Spaniards was punished for a misdeed by being tied to a stake and burnt. It was the Aztecs turn to be horrified. Cortes had a stake placed outside Montezuma's palace and then asked him to come and live with them. With such a hint, the emperor could not refuse. The emperor was now their hostage.

At this point, however, General Velasquez sent 18 ships after Cortes
with 900 men and much heavy artillery. Cortes was completely
outnumbered. He left a third of his men (only about 30 by now) in
the Aztec city and went to deal with the new threat.

The Spaniards were taken by surprise, and Cortes and his 70 men
and native friends won.

On his return Cortes found that his men had given the Aztecs
permission to hold a religious ceremony. The Spaniards had then
killed the worshippers. Aztec blood was said to have run down the
pavements like water after a heavy storm. A revolt by Montezuma's
brother had followed. As Cortes advanced into the city the Aztecs
cut off his retreat by smashing the bridges behind him. He was alone
in the middle of the city with his enemies all around him, and a
fortune in gold and precious objects in his possession.

The sad night – 'noche triste'

Cortes told his men to take with them only those treasures they
could easily carry. But the fever of treasure was too strong. They
stuffed gold bars into the tops of their boots, wrapped gold and silver
objects in jewelled cloth; they filled their jerkins with jewellery and
tied ornaments to their belts. They could hardly walk with the
weight of the gold.

At night they made their way through the sleeping streets taking
with them a makeshift bridge. The first causeway was bridged and
the Aztecs still slept. Men with their treasures scrambled to get
across but the weight of all the gold sank the bridge into the mud.
The Aztecs were alerted and the fighting began. Shrieks and screams
rent the night air as treasure and bodies were washed away. Not one
Spaniard escaped unwounded.

They finally escaped with their lives because the Aztecs tried to
recover the treasures from the water. At least a third of the
Spaniards died. They spent some time recovering, and then carried
on marching until 8 July 1520.

They were tired after their battles and they arrived in a vast open
valley, their only way of escape. The valley was completely filled
with at least 20,000 Aztec warriors, the chiefs in their shimmering
cloaks with their dyed feathers showing up brilliantly against the
white cotton tunics of the fighting men.
Sacrifice to a pagan god seemed the only end in store for the
Spaniards.

Then Cortes noticed that the most important chief sat in the centre of this fearsome force. He had a golden net for his banner and a badge on his back.

Spurring his horse forward through the masses of Aztecs, wielding his sword to either side, he hacked his way through his foe. His followers surged behind him. Straight to the chieftain he rode, ran him through with his lance and held the badge aloft.

With their leader killed the Aztecs fled.

Cortes went back to the Aztec capital some time later but the gold was gone. It has not been found to this day. He returned to Spain after ruling Mexico for some years, but he died without money. One of the most spectacular treasure hunts in history had done him no good.

3 Treasures of mystery

The land of Eldorado

Cortes was only one of the Spanish adventurers. The Spaniards had been given licence to explore the New World to the west of a line drawn on the map by Pope Alexander VI in 1493. The Portuguese were to explore to the east of the line. The explorers soon heard stories of a fabulous place where splendid festivals were held every year. The chieftain *El Dorado* (in Spanish it means 'The Gilded One') was said to cover himself in turpentine and then smear his body with gold dust. He dived – shining and glinting in the sun like a great golden rocket – into a lake. His followers then threw gold into the lake as well. The chieftain was first thought to live in a town near Bogota, Colombia, and searches were made by the Spanish, the Portuguese and the Germans to try to find him. In 1538 the Spanish from Peru and the Germans from Venezuela actually met each other somewhere near Bogota in their attempts to find the gilded chieftain. One Spaniard even claimed to have been entertained by El Dorado in a city near Omagua.

The searches, however, never found him, but the myths of a golden city which was called El Dorado grew and grew. Among those who tried to find the place was the Englishman, Sir Walter Raleigh. In 1603 the Portuguese actually put the words 'El Dorado' on a map: they reckoned it lay in what is now the Guianas. None of these explorers had any real luck in finding El Dorado, and nowadays it is thought that the Gilded One was probably a chief who had lived at least a hundred years before the Europeans ever set foot in the New World. He had probably been conquered by another native tribe and only his memory lived on in legend.

The well of Yum Chac

The Mayas were, like the Aztecs, one of the great civilizations of
America that had grown up before the arrival of the Europeans.
It was in discovering one of their great lost cities in the jungle of
the Yucatan that a British archaeologist, Edward Thompson, was
able to prove that such legends as that of El Dorado were founded
partly in fact.

The city was called Chichen Itza and a Spaniard, Diego de Landa,
had described some of the terrible rituals that had been carried
out there in the time of the Mayas. He had said that there was a
well that was sacred to the god called Yum Chac. In times of drought,
offerings to the god were thrown into the well. Beautiful young
girls, gold, household utensils and fine ornaments all found their
way into the water. Once the muffled cries of the victims had
stopped echoing around the walls of the well, onlookers knew that
the sacrificed people would never rise to the surface of the stagnant
slimy water again.

Edward Thompson found the sacred well and began to clear it out.
It was a difficult task, for the well was really a pool, 180 feet (54·6 m)
across. Soundings of the water suggested that it was 80 feet (24·2 m)
deep. Thompson dredged it day after day. His workmen thought him
mad, but Thompson believed the account of the Spaniard. Often
the water looked like blood, thick and clotting, because a red flower
and its seed capsules floated on the surface.

At last the efforts were rewarded. From the bottom of the well came
an amazing array of treasures; gold and copper, precious jade and
many other objects. Most horrible of all were the skulls. All but
one were of young girls who had died to please the fearsome rain-god
Yum Chac.

The land of Prester John

In the Middle Ages, long before El Dorado was thought of, people
were excited by tales of another fabulous land of gold – the land of
Prester John. This man was supposed to be a Christian king who
lived somewhere in the East. It was a time when the Christian
West frequently made crusades against the people of the East who
were not Christians. The East was the source of all their luxuries.
Spices were needed to make meat more tasty, and brocades, silks,
and gold and silver objects were traded. It is not surprising that

Westerners were able to believe in a rich kingdom in the Orient. The Crusaders' wish to regain the Holy Land was often only part of their reason for fighting, greed for power or glory and gold was as important. Thousands of innocent men, women and children were horribly killed and their villages looted during these 'Holy' wars. King Richard I of England spent little more than one year out of the eleven he was on the throne living in his own country. He preferred the rigours and glories of a life spent campaigning. During this period of neglect, his country suffered almost as many ills as the victims in the Holy Land.

The letter from Prester John

In 1165, during this time of violence and injustice, several Christian leaders are reported to have received a letter from *Prester John*.

The letter said that the land of Prester John (whose name means 'Presbyter John' or 'Priest John') abounded in milk and honey. It was a country without avarice, greed, cruelty or flattery. No robbers lived there, and there were no vices. All the people were religious and many of Prester John's staff were churchmen (his butler, for instance, was an archbishop). It was, in short, a sort of heaven-on-earth and very different from the Europe of the Middle Ages.

Nobody had actually been to this land, or met Prester John, so no doubt the European leaders were surprised to receive the letter. After eleven years, Pope Alexander III finally got round to replying and he sent off a letter which he addressed to the 'Illustrious and Magnificent King of the Indies and Beloved Son of Christ'. Presumably it was passed from diplomat to messenger to trader along the route east, just like all the exports.

Prester John was heard of no more, but tales of the idyllic kingdom he ruled were exaggerated and passed around. This was a time when there were no newspapers or TV or radio, so stories took a long time to get round. People began to say that Prester John came from India.

Then, in 1221, more news came of the land where no vice was known. A great king had won a victory over the Muslims. The victor was, it was said, a 'King David of India', a son or perhaps a grandson of the mighty Prester John. Explorers tried to find out who the king was. Several said that they had found him, but each time they named somebody different. By the fourteenth century, searches had moved to Ethiopia where news of another Christian king had confused the explorers. As usual with stories of untold riches, the searches were in vain. It is odd to think that hundreds of years later we know more about Prester John than the people of the Middle Ages did.

The whereabouts of Prester John

Nowadays we know where the land of Prester John is, but it cannot be put on any map. It was imaginary, even from the start. There never was, on this earth, a great king of a land without vice.

The writer of the letter made many mistakes that a real Prester John would not have made, for instance he used words that Prester John would not have used. The letter was a fake. It was probably sent to the Christian kings in the hope that they would do something about the misery and ills of their own countries. It is no wonder that Pope Alexander III did not receive a reply to his letter. So strong was the belief in the magical kingdom, however, that the victory by the 'king David' was probably a story made up about a victory won by Ghengis Khan over the Muslims.

King Solomon

The Bible tells us that King Solomon of Israel was well known for his wisdom and the power of his kingdom. Solomon's court was famous far and wide and people came to visit him and bring him gifts. His power was so great that the Queen of Sheba came to see his court for herself. She asked him many questions and when Solomon had answered her she gave him 120 talents of gold (a talent is a man-load or about 60 pounds [27·22 kg]), and many spices and precious stones. Then she returned to her own country.

According to the Bible, Solomon's income was six hundred, three score and six (666) talents of gold. He had 200 small shields made out of beaten gold, and 300 full-size shields, each with three pounds (1·36 kg) of beaten gold in it. After the departure of the Queen of Sheba he had a throne made out of ivory inlaid with gold. All his drinking cups were of gold, and his navy brought back gold, silver, ivory, apes and peacocks each year. Each year, too, people brought him gifts of gold and silver drinking vessels, armour, garments, spices, horses and mules.

Like many stories of fabulous riches, this tale of Solomon was probably exaggerated. It is thought that he was not nearly so great a king as the Bible suggests. He got his treasures by taxing his people heavily and making them unhappy. He lived between about 975 and 937 BC, and when he died his kingdom split up and his riches were scattered. No one has found his treasures, and they were probably melted down hundreds of years ago. However, they may one day come to light from a buried hiding place.

The golden statue of the Queen of Sheba

Nothing further was heard of the Queen of Sheba. The country she ruled over is now in the Yemen (south-west Arabia) and was called Saba. It is one of the least friendly and least productive areas of the world. It is amazing to think that 2,000 years ago it was a land of plenty, rich from trade.

She was one of several monarchs in Arabia, but her country was certainly the most prosperous. It grew rich by trading myrrh and frankincense with Egypt. The people of Saba lived in cities, and about 150 years after the time of Solomon they learned to write.

The Queen of Sheba's capital was probably modern *Ma'rib*, and intrepid explorers have tried to find out more about it, and perhaps discover the truth behind the legends of the Queen of Sheba's wealth. Until the nineteenth century, the Yemen was closed to outsiders. When the first explorers went there they found that the incense trade had dried up two thousand years before – when the Western world became Christian almost no incense was needed, and Saba had become poor again. For the first explorers it was like stepping back in time, for the rulers were despots who kept slaves and punished them by cutting off their hands, feet or even their heads.

Progress was slow because of the dangers from such hostile rulers. In 1869 Joseph Halery disguised himself as a Jew and travelled the country widely. But it was not until 1951 that a young American fossil hunter, Wendell Philips, got permission to dig at Ma'rib. There he investigated the temple of 'Ilmuqah. He found a huge hall over 80 feet (24·2 m) long and 66 feet (20 m) wide which had once had a roof held up by columns. It could have been the palace of the rulers of Sheba. Sadly, just as the investigations were getting under way, the local ruler decided that the diggers were trying to loot the ruins. He made their life very difficult by demanding copies of every single thing they found.

After a while the diggers realized that the ruler was plotting to kill
them. They were usually taken to the site from their camp in several
lorries, with armed Yemeni 'helpers' who were really guards. They
found that there was not enough gas in the tanks to take the lorries
very far into the desert, if they tried to escape. So they siphoned the
petrol into one lorry and in the morning the entire party squeezed
into the one vehicle with the Yemeni guards hanging on outside.
When they reached the ruins of Ma'rib the lorry slowed down and
the Yemeni guards jumped off, expecting the diggers to get out too.
Instead of stopping, the lorry accelerated into the desert, much to
the surprise of the guards. The diggers got completely away despite
the following gunshots.

The story was given out by the Yemeni ruler that the diggers had
been trying to smuggle out a gold statue of the Queen of Sheba
which they had found. They denied this, and certainly such a
statue has never come to light. The dig at the Queen's capital might
well yield great treasures if it is ever started again.

King Solomon's mines

The Emperors of Ethiopia traced their ancestry back to a certain
Menelik, who was supposed to be the son of Solomon and the Queen
of Sheba. When Africa was first being explored by men such as
Livingstone, Baker and Grant, the continent had been a mystery to
Europeans for thousands of years. The tribes were not friendly, the
land difficult to cross. Once the interior had been reached, however,
the traders and prospectors, hunters and settlers soon flocked in.
They were greedy for riches, land or power. There were already
many stories about the wealth of the continent. The Portuguese
traders had brought back tales of a ruler in Africa with a palace
covered in plates of gold. Among the many ruins were said to be the
remains of King Solomon's mines, and other ruins were claimed as
the palace of Menelik. A treasure hunt followed. Many ruins were
wrecked by the hunters who hoped to gain gold and valuable objects.
One group, the 'Ancient Ruins Company', specialized in destroying
remains merely to find the valuables they contained. Much of the
African past was smashed for small amounts of loot.

The mines of Solomon were never found in Africa, and the palace
supposed to belong to Menelik was proved to belong to a much
later period. Further excavations were made in the Gulf of Aqaba,

off the Red Sea. A blast furnace and copper slag were found that were first thought to be the mines of Solomon. Later studies proved that these too were not used during Solomon's reign. The fabulous mines where Solomon's riches were said to be hidden are still a mystery. Maybe one day they will come to light.

The land of Punt

The ancient Egyptians had their own dreams of unlimited treasures – the land of Punt. It was a land where there were many riches and, what was more, people had been there and come back laden with luxuries and treasures. In about 3,000 BC the pharaoh Sahu-Re had sent some of his men to Punt. The adventurers returned with 80,000 measures of myrrh and 6,200 weights of electrum as well as

Queen Hatshepsut (kneeling)

costly woods, and dwarves, who were used in dances in the Egyptian temples. The Egyptians traded far afield for their luxuries. They bought their incense from southern Arabia, but the prices were high and it was cheaper to go to Punt. Egyptian life needed sweet-smelling nards from the Ganges, cinnamon from the Himalayas, muslin from Ceylon, silk from China, tortoiseshell from Malacca, and indigo, pepper, diamonds, emeralds, sapphires and lapis lazuli from India. The lure of cheap treasure was therefore great to the Egyptians who had to pay highly for the luxuries.

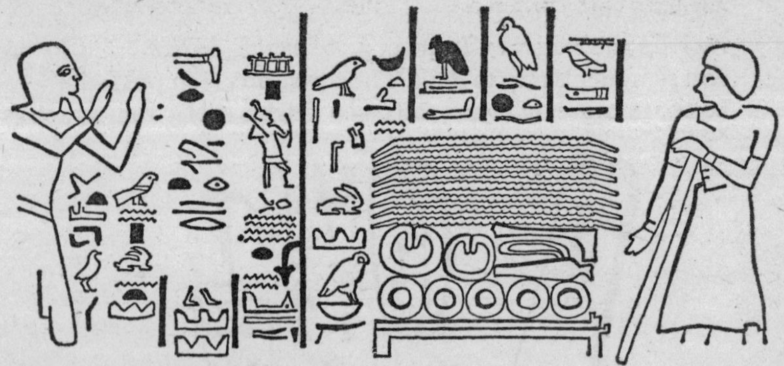

Egyptian trade mission meeting the chief of Punt

In 1493 BC the queen of Egypt was Hatshepsut. She had a stormy life (and was probably murdered by her own husband in the end), but in this year she decided to send some men to Punt. The previous expedition had taken place 750 years previously, so it was time for another visit. Furthermore, the mines in Upper Egypt had given out a long time before. As expected, the five galleys returned laden with goods. There were incense and ebony, apes, dogs and leopard skins; the trip had been a great success.

The mystery about Punt is not that the Egyptians could not find it, but that today we do not know where it was. All we know is that the Egyptians sailed south from the Red Sea and came back laden with treasure. A princess of Punt is pictured on the walls of the temple at Dahr el Bahri. She has a very fat bottom, particularly compared to the slim Egyptians, which suggests she was a Hottentot. There is another picture which shows the Egyptian mission meeting Pairohu, the chief of Punt. In front of them are beads on a table. There have been some clues which suggest that Punt may have been somewhere near the Zambesi, but nobody can be certain.

Modern treasures of mystery

Some treasure hunts are still in progress. As late as 1977 the
Russians asked to see a list of art items found in the house of a
Dutchman suspected of war crimes. They wanted to check if the
items were on their own lists of things which had mysteriously
disappeared during World War II.

Incredible numbers of treasures were taken during World War II –
Hitler, Goering and Mussolini all made private art collections, and
novelists have written many thrillers about what might have
happened to their fortunes. In Germany the orders were very
simple – no Jewish person was allowed to pawn or acquire in any
way any object of gold, platinum, silver, precious stones or pearls,
and they were allowed only to sell such articles to the state. This
meant in effect that their treasures were taken from them.

Personal treasures are often lost. Usually they are simply shared
among lots of people, but there are many stories of the great treasure
supposed to belong to the *Romanov* family who were the last rulers
of Russia. It is said that a fortune is hidden deep in a secret,
numbered account in a Swiss Bank, but nobody has ever found out
if this is true. The Romanovs met their death tragically. The Tsar,
Tsarina and the prince and princesses were all said to have been
shot in 1917. Anna Anderson claimed to be the princess Anastasia
who had escaped, but her case has never been proved. It has been
suggested that the entire family escaped death, and are living
unknown but safe elsewhere in the world. The family and their
treasure still cause excitement and interest.

No matter how much evidence is found to suggest the opposite,
there is always a suspicion at the back of people's minds that
perhaps treasures really do exist.

4 Haunted treasures

The Egyptians believed that when they died they would need everything they had used in their lifetime. Therefore they buried their dead with all the comforts, necessities and luxuries that they had enjoyed in life. Even food went into the tombs. The richest tombs were those of the rulers, the pharaohs. Each pharaoh spent most of his reign ordering the building of his tomb, and the pyramids are among the most magnificent burial chambers ever made. The walls were painted with scenes from the pharaoh's life. Food, drink, chairs, tables, cushions and treasures accompanied the coffin. The dead pharaoh's body was prepared for burial with a complicated process to preserve it. The innards were removed and put into separate jars and the brain was removed through the nostrils. Then the body was treated with many preserving liquids. Many *mummies*, as these bodies are called, have been well preserved to this day and can be seen in many museums.

The curses of the tomb

The thought of preserving a human body and then entombing it in a vast stone pyramid, sealed from the world by doors and false entrances to guard its treasures, has fired the imagination of many writers. The Egyptian tombs often have 'curses' written over the doors, which threaten to bring the wrath of the gods on anyone who disturbs the peace of the dead person. It is not surprising that Egyptian mummies and their tombs sound very scary. Many stories have grown up about mummies haunting people who have opened their tombs, or taken their treasures. The British Museum Egyptian room has long been thought haunted, for it contains many mummies of important Egyptians. Very few, if any, of these stories can be proved, but people are still fascinated to think that someone who died thousands of years ago might seek vengeance on tomb robbers.

The boy pharaoh with the golden mask

The most famous mummy is that of the young king Tutankhamun.
He became pharaoh when he was only 11 years old and he died
before he was 20. His reign was not very important and his name
would have been almost unknown if it had not been for his splendid
tomb. It was so rich, and there were so many curses to those who
broke down its doors, that a story of a curse has grown up about
Tutankhamun.

The story begins in 1914, at the start of the First World War, when
the Egyptian government gave Howard Carter and Lord Caernarvon
permission to dig in the sand dunes. They were both remarkable
men. Lord Caernarvon was a sportsman, a collector and a keen
traveller (he owned the third automobile to be licensed in Britain).
When he was young he had an accident that left him in bad health,
so in 1903 he left for milder climates and soon met up with Howard
Carter.

Howard Carter interested Lord Caernarvon in digging up the past.
He was a strong character who went through many difficulties to
follow his interest in the past. During the First World War,
archaeological digs in Egypt were ruined by gangs of organized and
ruthless tomb robbers. They opened up the tombs of the ancient
rulers and then traded the valuable, often priceless objects. At the
same time they destroyed archaeological evidence.

The midnight robbers

There is a story that two rival gangs fought a pitched battle in the
sandy Valley of the Kings in 1916. The winning gang then started
to loot the tombs, no doubt thinking that they would not be
disturbed for some time. They had bargained without Howard
Carter. In the moonlight he and a few workmen climbed over the
Kurna Hills and at midnight arrived at the edge of a steep cliff. A
rope dangled over the edge into the darkness. From the bottom of the
cliff came the scraping and heaving noises of the robbers digging up
their booty. Working silently in the silvery moonlight Carter cut the
rope, secured one of his own and then shinned down to face the
robbers alone. The meeting must have been an exciting one. The
seven or eight men had already got rid of their rivals by force, and
must have thought themselves free to steal the treasures at night.
Instead they found themselves face to face with the moonlit figure of

Howard Carter, firmly grasping their only means of escape from the
bottom of the cliff. No doubt they were taken aback by his boldness,
for they quickly decided to cut their losses and leave their loot.
They climbed up the rope to freedom.

It was not for several years after this event that Howard Carter
and his patron Lord Caernarvon found the treasure of Tutankhamun.
They were digging near the tomb of the pharaoh Ramses VI. They
uncovered an area under the huts used by the workmen who had
built Ramses' tomb. It was a great stroke of luck that they found
anything at all, because the entire sandy Valley of the Kings had
been well sifted by the many archaeologists and tomb robbers over
the years. In November 1922 Carter dug under the workmen's huts
and he found a sealed door in the rubble. A hole was bored, a torch
shone through and, looking inside, Carter knew he had found a
rare thing. Here was a tomb that had not been broken into by
modern robbers. The ancient seals were unbroken.

Lord Caernarvon rushed back from England and the search
continued. They found that the tomb had been broken into by
ancient Egyptians and resealed several times. The last seals were
unbroken so perhaps there was something left inside.

The wall of solid gold

The team opened the door and went down a long passage, past
another sealed door, and they finally found themselves in a room
filled with a jumble of furniture and everyday objects. Three
sealed doors led off the room. Evidently the ancient tomb robbers
had been disturbed. They had merely rifled through the furniture
before they had been hauled off for punishment, or had been
frightened away.

One of the sealed doors was opened in front of Egyptian officials.
They scraped a small hole and pushed a torch into the darkness.

Their eyes were met by a wall of solid gold! It was an incredible
find. Not only was the tomb still as it had been left thousands of
years before, but inside were splendid treasures.

In fact, the wall of solid gold was the side of a sacred box or shrine
which filled a room 17 feet (5·1 m) long, 11 feet (3·3 m) wide. It was
covered with gold, inlaid with panels of blue faience (a type of glass).
At one end a pair of folding doors opened on to another shrine, and
a third, and then a fourth which had beautiful goddesses to guard it.

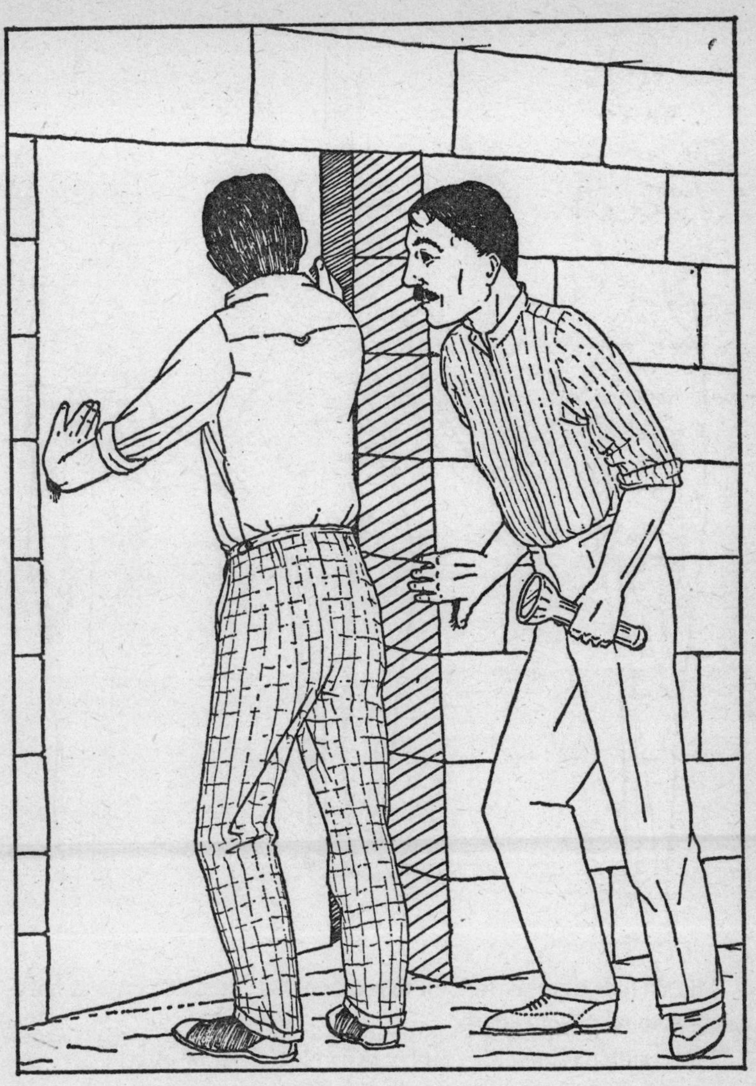

S—BT—B

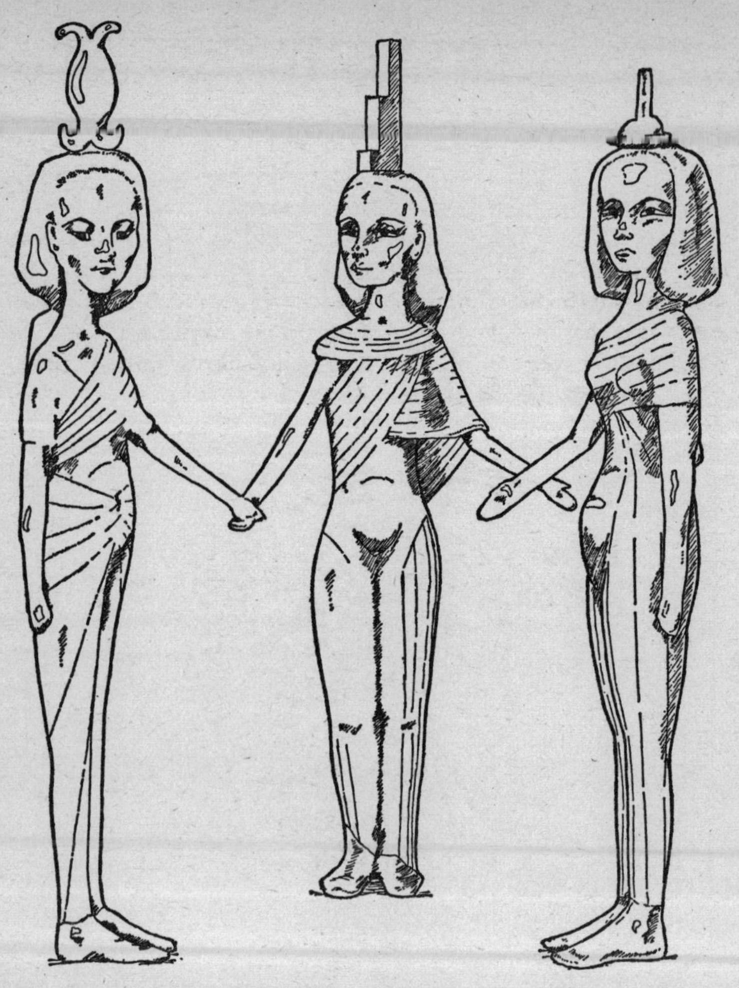

The shrines were so difficult to remove that it took 84 days of hard effort to take them apart.

The young pharaoh himself lay in a golden-yellow quartz sarcophagus on a golden stand. The lid was rose quartz and inside was a golden effigy of the king. The face was of pure gold. The eyes were made of aragonite and the eyebrows were of obsidian, two beautiful stones. There were three coffins in all, one inside each other. The innermost was of solid gold about 0·2 inches (0·51 cm) thick. It was truly a buried treasure fit for a king.

The walls of the room were painted with scenes from the young king's life and the objects in the tomb were all costly and beautiful.

The story did not end when the treasures were taken to Cairo museum. Lord Caernarvon died before the dig was finished and a story grew up that the boy king was taking vengeance on everyone connected with the dig. Every time someone died, the story grew. Fortunately the curse story does not stand up to close examination. Many people seemed to have escaped the curse and have lived long and happy lives. Since everyone must die some time, it is only too easy to say that they did so because of a curse. Even so, it is not possible to be sure that the young king is not taking his revenge on those who disturbed his peace.

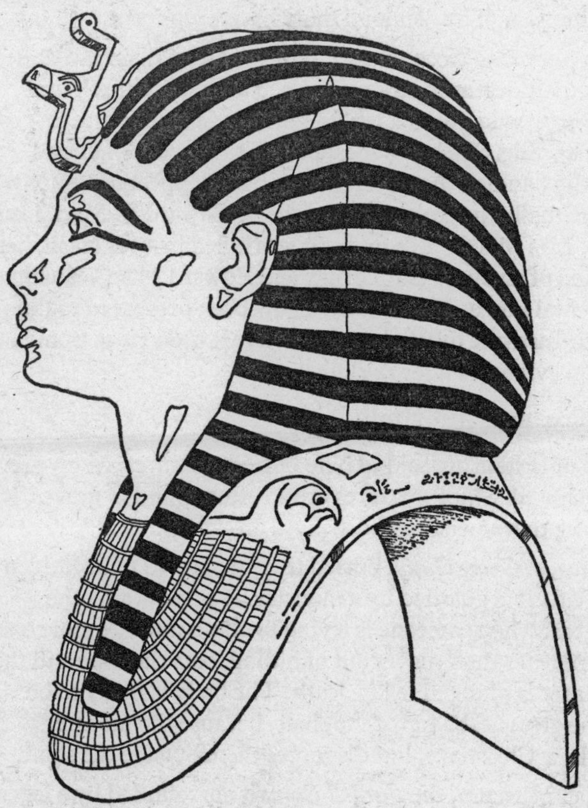

The golden mask of Tutankhamun

The curse of the Hope diamond

The Hope diamond has traditionally brought bad luck, despite its name. This fine blue stone was once mounted in the forehead of a statue of the god Rama Rita, in India. A French gem expert, Jean Baptiste Tavernier, somehow managed to get hold of it and the diamond was sold to Louis XIV of France in 1668. Five years later it was recut into the shape of a heart. When the French crown jewels were stolen, the diamond was not recovered. It seemed to have disappeared without trace.

Then, in 1830, a blue stone appeared on the market in London and was bought by Sir Thomas Hope. It is now thought that the diamond sold by Tavernier and the Hope diamond (as this was then called) were the same gem. The diamond must have been recut.

People who came into close contact with the Hope diamond do seem to have met their deaths in strange ways. Tavernier himself was torn to pieces by wild dogs. It is said that Marie Antoinette owned the gem for a while. She was beheaded. The Antwerp diamond merchant who handled the stone when it had reappeared committed suicide. Eventually the stone was bought by Edward B. MacClean for his wife. Mrs MacClean's first son was killed in a car crash, her daughter died of an overdose of drugs and Edward MacClean himself died in a mental home. The stone has now been presented to the Smithsonian Institute in Washington where it is on view. Some say it glints in an evil way under the lights.

Haunted treasures in Britain

Many areas of Britain are said to hide buried treasures. Many are said to be haunted. Since treasures are so often found in graves, it is not surprising that stories of ghosts have grown up.

On Dartmoor, at *Chaw Gully*, buried treasure is said to be hidden in a mine shaft. It is guarded by a monster. A raven warns the terrifying beast when someone is trying to climb into the mine on a rope. The monster then rushes out of hiding, cuts the rope and the treasure hunter is plunged to his death. The body is likely to be found on the grass at the top of the shaft, because the monster cannot swallow Christians, but disgorges them outside the shaft.

In the British Museum, the *Fardell Stone* is surrounded by a legend of buried treasure. It came from Fardell House in Devon where a field between the house and a bridge is said to be barren. Apparently in the field is buried treasure, guarded by a young lady. She wears a rustling dress of silk and glides up and down the road in a ghostly fashion.

In *Dobb Park Castle*, near Otley, Yorkshire, it is said that a dog with three heads guards a treasure hidden under the stairs.

At *Roslin Castle*, East Lothian, Scotland, a lady is supposed to guard a million pounds hidden in the castle vault. She is fast asleep like the sleeping beauty and can only be woken when a knight named Wilson breaks the charm by blowing a trumpet call and claiming the treasure.

Stokesay Castle in Shropshire has a sad legend of haunted treasure. Apparently the surrounding area once belonged to two giants who lived on the two hills each side of the castle. They kept their treasures in the castle vault and whenever one wanted to take out some money he would call across and the other giant would throw him the key. Sadly, one day the key fell by accident into the moat and was never found. One giant was so heartbroken that he died. The treasure is supposed to be guarded by a raven until the key is found.

It is best not to go to *Ruborough Camp* in Somerset hoping to dig up treasure. Although the legend says that buried treasure can be dug up when the moon is full, a ghostly chariot and horse will run you over.

Markyate Cell, Hertfordshire, was the home of wicked Lady Ferrers, a 17th-century highwaywoman. She used to leave her home at the dead of night by a secret door, and then she would waylay travellers. When she had robbed them she would tie them to a tree and return home to her life as a lady. One night, however, she was shot and died on her way back. The treasures she must have taken from her victims have never been found, but there is a rhyme to help hunters:

Near the cell there is a well,
Near the well there is a tree,
And 'neath the tree the treasure be.

5 Accidental discoveries and excavations

Ever since the Great Wall was built, China has seemed a land of mystery to outsiders. The Great Wall, a 3,000 mile (4,827 km) -long barrier, was built to protect the Chinese from the fierce nomads who often attacked them. The most famous were the Hsiung-nu, who were later feared in Europe where they were known as the Huns.

The name China comes from the first dynasty to rule over a Chinese Empire – the Ch'in. Under their emperor, the Ch'in-Shih-Huang, the Chinese joined up the sections of the Great Wall they had already built and became cut off from the rest of the world. Only a few brave explorers managed to travel inside China.

The sea of mercury

The Emperors of China were buried with great ceremony and many fantastic treasures were put in their tombs. It was said that the first Emperor was laid in a bronze coffin and buried in a huge mound surrounded by a sea of mercury. The dead man was defended by booby traps that fired arrows. The tomb is known, but has not been properly excavated. It will probably contain great treasures if it has not already been looted.

The Ch'in dynasty was soon replaced by that of the Han, who ruled China from 206 BC to 220 AD. By this time the Chinese had become less bloodthirsty in their burial habits – they no longer sacrificed people to bury with the dead, but made little figurines instead. The most important burials were those of the imperial family and one of these, found accidentally, gained world-wide fame because of its rich treasures.

One dark night in 1966 a patrol of the People's Liberation Army stumbled across some boulders that had fallen down a mountainside.

They looked more closely and discovered that they had found a hole in the roof of an ancient and very rich tomb that had been cut into the rock of the mountain. They lowered themselves into the tomb and peered around by torchlight. In the dim glow the glint of jade, gold and lacquered ornaments, silver and bronze, met their eyes. The tomb was exactly as it had been left 2,100 years ago.

Archaeologists, helped by the soldiers and local people, excavated the treasures. They soon discovered that the tomb was that of Liu Sheng, brother of the emperor of China, Wu-ti. The dead man was the prince of Chung Shang province. He had governed for about 40 years until his death in about 113 BC.

The wall of iron

When Liu Sheng had been buried, the entrance to the tomb had been sealed off with two brick walls. The space between them had been filled with molten iron, a very difficult feat for the time. It was an effective seal. The diggers had trouble climbing through the roof as they brought out the treasures, and in the end they were forced to use a method of removing the wall that no archaeologist would ever use by choice. They blew it up with dynamite!

The tomb of Prince Liu Sheng, full of treasures

The entrance to the tomb led to a passage which ended in a large room in which thousands of bronze jars and other offerings had been neatly laid out. The room with the coffin was entered by a small door, and a curved passage allowed people to walk around it. All this was hewn from solid rock.

Two tunnels led from the passage. In these lay the skeletons of 16 horses and 11 dogs, along with 6 carriages, and food and wine. There was a grindstone which a horse had pulled round to grind grain to make into bread if its dead owner had felt hungry. The horse's bones lay beside the stone it had once dragged.

The diggers thought that if there was one tomb there might be more. They searched the opposite hillside, leaving no stone unturned, and their efforts were rewarded. Another tomb, in perfect condition, came to light. In this Tan Wan, the wife of Liu Sheng, had been buried. This lady is now better known as the *Princess of Jade*.

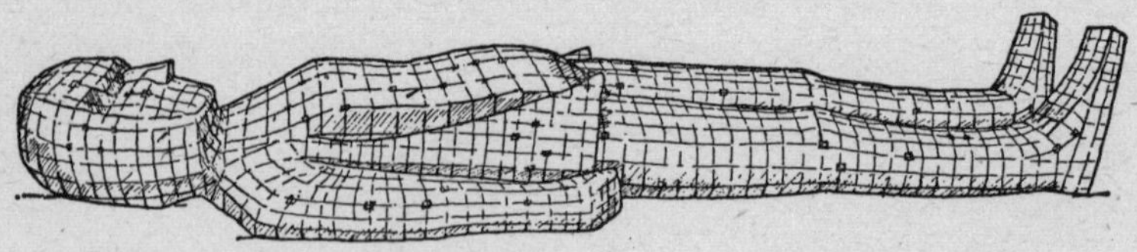

Both Tan Wan and Liu Sheng were completely covered in jade suits when they were buried. It was known that important Chinese people were sometimes buried in costumes made of this beautiful, translucent, hard, green stone, but no complete suits have ever been found except for those of Liu Sheng and Tan Wan. The suits were in themselves fantastic treasures, even without the 2,800 other objects found in Liu Sheng's tomb. Each suit had been made in pieces before the prince and princess had died, and each was a perfect fit. Each of the 2,156 pieces of jade in Tan Wan's suit and the 2,690 pieces in her husband's suit had been separately carved, then four little holes had been drilled at the corners so that they could be strung together with lengths of gold thread. Even a skilled jade-worker would take over 10 years to make one outfit, and obviously the rock-cut tomb and the jade suits were begun long before the prince and princess died. Jade could not be found in China, and had to be brought from East Turkestan in Central Asia. For the Chinese, it was the symbol of everlasting life.

An 'eternal fidelity' lamp from the Prince's tomb

Only the imperial family were normally allowed to use gold thread in their jade suits, so the Prince and Princess of Jade must have been in the emperor's favour to be granted this honour.

The tombs of the Scythian blood drinkers

Great treasures have been found in Russia. Few have been more exciting than those uncovered in the tombs of the Scyths, whose barbaric rituals have amazed later ages. The Scyths were wandering tribesmen who travelled widely in the Russian plain around 3,000 years ago. They left no houses, for they lived in tents and carried their few belongings around with them. Their luggage consisted only of a few portable tables, cushions and hangings, tools, cooking pots and cauldrons.

The Scyths could not read or write, but they could ride horses. It was this that gave them an advantage over the other wandering people who could not ride, and the civilized Chinese and Assyrians who drove in chariots.

A fierce Scyth

The Greeks thought the Scyths were a bunch of cowboys and said that they scalped their enemies and then drank their blood out of skulls. The Scyths certainly did lead exciting and dangerous lives much of the time.

The Scyths were a force to be reckoned with. The Persian king, Darius, decided to annoy his enemies, the Greeks, by cutting off their trade routes. To this end he decided to destroy the Scyths. No doubt he thought that gangs of people who could not read or write would be easy prey for the Persian army. He was wrong. The Persians crossed the Bosphorus, passed south-east Roumania, and then crossed the Danube river. They were now in the most desolate plain where only the toughest men were able to make a living. This was home ground for the Scyths. They split their forces into three groups and dared Darius to cross the plain. Deeper and deeper into the vast wasteland the Persian army followed the Scyths, until finally they crossed the Don and the Volga. They were miles from home. The tribesmen burnt all the lands round the Persians – they themselves did not care if the land was burnt since they did not depend on farm produce and if they got hungry they could simply move on to a plentiful supply of game, gathering up their few belongings on their horses. Finally Darius challenged them, calling

them cowards. The king of the Royal Scyths warned Darius:
'We have nothing to fear from you Persians, we do not have towns for
you to spoil. But if you damage our tombs, then you will find out
whether or not we are cowards.'

Sensibly, Darius did not put this to the test. He withdrew his
troops and went home.

The treasure tombs of the Scyths

The tombs that the Royal Scyth had challenged Darius to loot
were the only lasting mark the tribes left on the land. They housed
the greatest treasures – superb golden cauldrons from Greece, and
many golden trinkets. Like the Chinese and the Egyptians the Scyths
believed that a man should take as much as possible with him to the
afterlife when he died.

The burial rites seem very odd and cruel to our modern minds.
They varied the rites according to where they were living at the
time – in some places it was difficult to bury their dead because of
the frozen soil, and so they waited until the spring thaw to carry
out their rituals.

Sometimes the dead Scythian leader was taken in a cart with all his
jewels and clothes on a journey round his territory. This lasted
about 40 days, and during this time his burial mound was built.
The sight of the funeral procession must have been awe-inspiring.
The wailing Scyths tended to cut off their hair and even their ears,
and they waved rattles to show their grief.
Eventually they would halt, the chief would be buried, and the
wake (feast) would begin.

It was not for another year that the oddest event took place. On the
anniversary of the chief's death, the Scyths were said to kill 50
warriors and their horses. These were impaled on huge stakes so
they stood in a circle around the tomb guarding their dead chief.
It is not known how often these horrible rites were carried out, if at
all. One tomb was found to have three horse skeletons with their
heads near a stake. This suggests that there might be some truth
behind the legend.

Of all the treasures buried in the Scythian tombs the most
magnificent were of gold. Plunderers have often robbed the tombs
in the past, leaving only the skeletons of horses. One tomb that was
opened in 1913 contained no less than 200 sacrificed horses.

The Seven Brothers' Barrow lies near the Kuban river in Russia, and
was the burial place of a royal family of Scyths. They had been
traders with the Greeks despite their wandering way of life. Many
beautiful treasures were found in this tomb. It was a mound over
59 feet (18 m) high. As well as horse skeletons and human bones
there was leather armour with iron and bronze scales, some
decorated with gold leaf. The breast plate of the dead man was
decorated in silver and had a design of a deer suckling a fawn. The
man's clothing had been covered with gold plaques which had once
been sewn on. The threads had decayed and they lay around his
bones. Each one was very beautiful. There were three gold torcs
(neckrings) around his neck. The plaques showed pictures of
animals and some human heads. There was part of an ox on one, a
lion with its head turned backwards on another.
One showed a lion leaping with its jaws open,
others showed Greek gods.

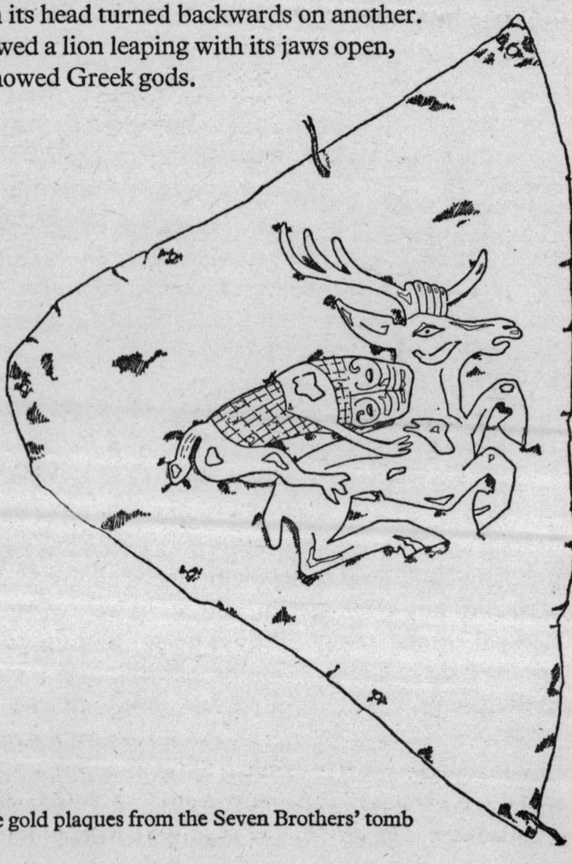

One of the gold plaques from the Seven Brothers' tomb

Near the human bones was a sword, and a spear and arrowhead.
There was a huge jug of silver, shaped like a horn with a lion's
head at the end. It was used for pouring out offerings to a god.
There was a goblet made of alabaster and a strainer . . . the list is
almost endless. Even the bridles of the horses were richly decorated.
The Scyths might have been cruel and savage, but the standards of
living of the richest must have been luxurious, even if they did live
in tents.

The treasure of the Queen of Sumer

The Queen of Sumer was dead. Her subjects and servants prepared
for the funeral in the ancient city of Ur, on the river Euphrates.
The funeral was to be a fitting burial for a great queen. Her followers
laid her body on a bier in the tomb. On her head was a fine headdress.

The Queen of Sumer
wearing her golden headdress,
golden earrings and pendant

It was made of three golden headbands from which hung golden
rings, golden beech leaves and golden flowers. Blue lapis lazuli
and red carnelian stones sparkled among the golden stems. In the
grave they also put her gold and silver treasures – golden cups,
jewellery, ornaments. The ceremonies required a large number of

people to take part. Two handmaidens crouched at the foot and head of the bier. Ladies of the court filed in, wearing their best clothes and their jewels. The court musician came with his harp.

At last the preparations were finished, but the people had not crowded into the tomb for a short ritual. They had dressed up in their best clothes to die. The Queen of Sumer was guarded by the Sumerians, even in death. For 5,000 years they lay in the tomb until Sir Leonard Woolley uncovered the tomb in 1927–9. It is thought that the people took poison in the grave.

Buried treasure was a lure even in those bygone days. The queen was buried close to the tomb of her husband who had died before her. In order to build her tomb the workers had to toil near the outer treasure chamber of her husband's tomb. It must have been full of fabulous treasures to judge by those that were found in the room where he was buried. The workers could not resist temptation. They broke into his treasure store and removed the valuables. Then they hid the hole they had made, with a large chest, in the queen's tomb.

The treasure ship

Over 1,300 years ago another funeral was in progress on the sandy river bank of the Deben in Suffolk, England. There was a wailing and moaning as the Saxons sent their dead king to his grave. The ship in which he had sailed during his life was dragged up the sandbank and half buried in a mound. Into the ship they placed the dead man's chain mail, his fine helmet, his sword and his shield. He had golden buckles with red garnets to decorate them, and a fine purse. There was a superb bowl and silver dishes. A huge dish of silver had been made in Byzantium and then traded across Europe until it reached the king. This was put into the grave too. The mound was then covered over and the Saxons left to start a new life with a new king.

Years passed and the treasure in the mound was forgotten. The wind and weather attacked the mound and it became smaller. In the seventeenth century robbers dug a hole through what they thought was the middle. They were intent on finding loot. They were disappointed and had to go away empty-handed. What they had thought was the centre of the mound was in fact one end, because the weather had made the mound much smaller. It was not until

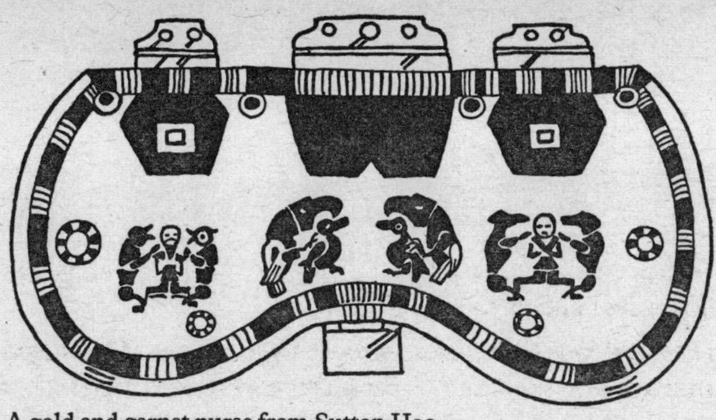

A gold and garnet purse from Sutton Hoo

1938 that the treasures were uncovered once more.
This mound and ten others were covered with bracken and ling
but the landowner, Mrs Edith May Pretty, was curious about them.
Archaeologists began to investigate the mound for her and the
results were spectacular.

The treasure found at this mound near the village of Sutton Hoo
was one of the most splendid ever found in Britain and is on view
in the British Museum.

The lavender field treasure

Another splendid treasure came to light by accident at Snettisham
in Norfolk, not far from the royal house of Sandringham.

A field of lavender was being deep-ploughed for the first time in
1948. On 12 November
Mr R. L. Williamson's
tractor turned up some
half hoops of coppery
metal which he
thought came from
a brass
bedstead.
Next day some
more tangled
metalwork came up –
it was like bits of green
string – and three days
later some green discs appeared.

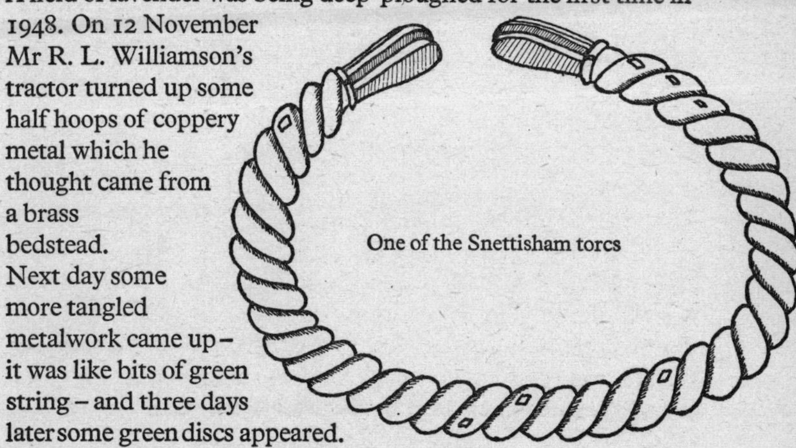

One of the Snettisham torcs

A week later, the director of the firm which grew the lavender saw the finds. He reported them to the Norfolk Research Committee. The discs turned out to be coins, some of the earliest ever made in this country. They were made even before the Romans arrived – over 2,000 years ago. Some were made of electrum, an alloy of gold and silver. The tubes turned out to be necklets (torcs) of gold. An inquest was held to decide whether the treasure belonged to the Crown. If it had been deliberately buried without the owner intending to return, for instance if it were in a grave, then it belonged to the finder. The first treasures to be discovered at Snettisham were declared Treasure Trove since it was thought that the owner had meant to come back for them. Excavations were carried out but very little else was found.

Then, in 1950, the plough turned up yet another treasure. This hoard of riches was found with a large number of iron nails all around it. This was all that remained of a wooden box. The hoard was evidently buried for safety at some time. Some gold coins were found standing on their sides – they had probably been in a leather pouch that had perished.

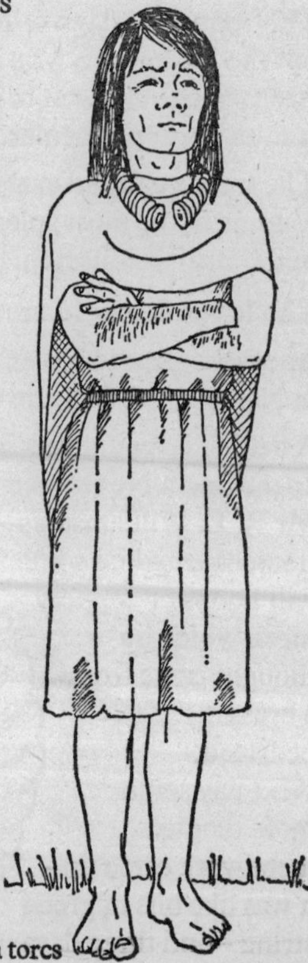

An Iron Age man wearing one of the Snettisham torcs

The plough that uncovered
two million pounds-worth of treasure

A farmer ploughing a field near Mildenhall in Suffolk, during the
wartime year of 1940, discovered the richest hoard to be found in
in Britain. The silverwork was estimated to be worth over £2 million.
The metal was worked into finely decorated dishes and spoons –
there were 30 pieces in all. The largest and most beautiful dish was
over two feet (0·6 m) in diameter and was covered in scenes from
Roman myths.

The treasure was probably buried by its owner during the third
century AD when the Roman Empire was torn by wars. No doubt
the owner felt that the silver would be safer in the ground than in
his own home. At any moment his house might be looted or his
lands taken away and the silver stolen. He no doubt intended to
return to dig it up again. For some reason he never came back –
perhaps he was killed in battle. We will never know. The treasure is
now in the British Museum.

6 Young people and treasure

Many young people have discovered great treasures – usually by accident. In 1976 nine-year-old Gary Fridd had a problem. He had been keeping tadpoles to watch them grow into frogs, but there was nobody to look after them over the Easter holidays. His teacher told him to let them go in the village stream where he lived at Gilling West, near Richmond in Yorkshire. He did, but went back that night to see if the tadpoles were still there. It was then that he found treasure.

Lying in a few inches of water he could see the glint of silver. He had found an iron sword, its hilt inlaid with silver. It had been lost in the stream by an Anglo-Saxon chief about a thousand years before. Experts valued it at £5,000 and declared it to be one of the finest swords of its period ever found in England. A Treasure Trove inquest was held, and it was decided that the sword belonged to the landowner, Lord Bolton, who generously allowed Gary to keep it.

The treasures of Priam

In 1829 a German boy of only six years old was given a beautiful book called *Jerrer's Illustrated History of the World*. Inside was a picture of an ancient Greek called Aeneas. He was carrying his aged father on his back, and leading his small son by the hand; the background was the burning city of Troy from which he was fleeing. The city of Troy had been beseiged for ten years. Heroes and princes and kings of Greece had all taken part, trying to win back the beautiful Helen who had been taken away from her family by Paris. In the story a great treasure was important. It belonged to Priam, the king of Troy.

The little boy, Heinrich Schliemann, was spell-bound by the story. He began to dream that one day he would find Troy.

It was to be 40 years before his dream came true.

When he was 14 Heinrich worked as a grocer's apprentice and his dream seemed far off. In 1841 he signed on as a cabin boy on a ship bound for Venezuela, but the ship was caught in a storm before it reached the Atlantic, and he soon found himself in Amsterdam. He became an office boy and started learning languages. Within two years he could speak English, French, Dutch, Spanish, Portuguese and Italian!

But the dream of finding Troy was yet far away. He worked his way up in the office and his work took him on many travels – to Russia and later to America. He arrived in the United States during the gold rush. Instead of rushing out with his gold pan like so many others, he kept his head and opened a bank for gold dealing. He was becoming a very rich man.

His travels began to take him nearer Greece. In 1856 he sailed through the islands and stopped at some. Within twelve years he was very rich indeed – rich enough to stop work and devote himself to the costly whim of searching for Troy.

The following year he married a young and beautiful Greek called Sophia. Together, armed with a book by the ancient Greek writer Homer, they ignored the laughter and anger of scholars, and started digging at the spot that Schliemann had decided was the site of Troy. He had a hundred workers to help him as well as the beautiful Sophia. Ruin after ruin was uncovered by the spades and the remains of nine cities were discovered. Each city had been built, had decayed, and had been pulled down, and a new series of buildings put up on the debris, in exactly the way cities are rebuilt today. The problem lay in deciding which of the stone walls and foundations were those that imprisoned the beautiful Helen of Troy so many years before. They were so near the truth and still there was no proof.

The golden jewellery

Schliemann set 15 July 1873 as the last day of his dig. In the early hours of the hot morning on 14 July, one day before the last, Sophia and Heinrich had got up to supervise the diggings. They were 28 feet (8·5 m) below ground surface and in the dust and debris they saw gold.

Without any hesitation Schliemann dismissed his workers.

Here was the gold of Troy. The 40-year-old dream was ended.
He hacked feverishly at the stones, pulling the rubble aside and then
wrapped the treasures in Sophia's shawl. There were golden diadems
and brooches, plates, chains, buttons and threads. He put the 3,000-
year-old earrings and pendants on his wife – in his eyes she was
another Helen of Troy. Eventually they managed to smuggle the
treasures out of the country – the story goes that at one point they
had to wrap them in Sophia's red flannel knickers.

When the scholars finally settled down to studying Schliemann's
finds they discovered that the gold he had found was not the gold
of Priam at all. The Troy that Helen had been carried to was the
second or third city that the diggers had found. Schliemann had
dug straight through the city he had wanted to find.

Golden cuttlefish and golden masks

Troy had been rich, but the hopes that Schliemann had had as a
young boy were rekindled. This time he went to Mycenae, the city
in Greece that had been described by the Greek writer Homer as
golden.

Since the remains had never been covered over by soil or sand, he
had no difficulty in finding the city. He did find a fantastic treasure,
however. Diadems of gold and gold leaves and ornaments abounded.

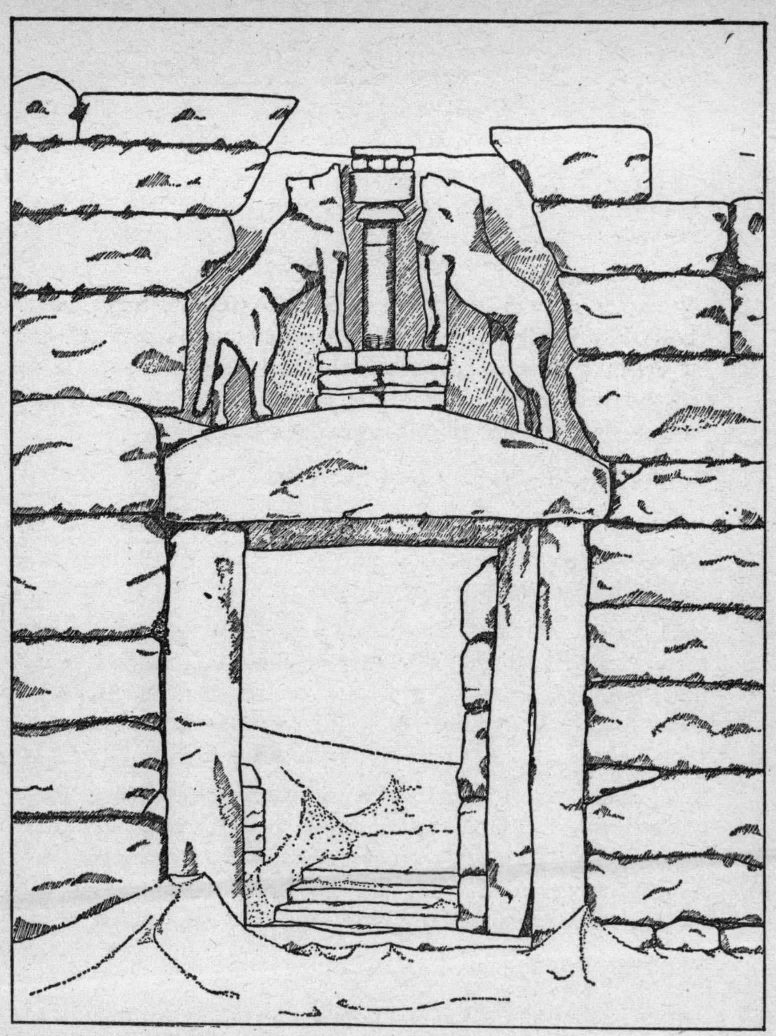

The lion gate at Mycenae, where Schliemann dug his great treasures

There were golden cuttlefish and flowers, golden animals and masks, and breastplates of the shining metal.

Schliemann offered these treasures to the Greek government and then to the French and then to the Russians. Unfortunately for these countries Schliemann was now such a businessman that he asked £40,000–£50,000 for them. Nobody was prepared to pay such a sum and at last they found their way to Berlin.

Schliemann died and the First World War came and went. The golden treasures from Troy and Mycenae were taken first to the Prussian State Bank and then to the Berlin Zoo for safety. The beautiful pottery that Schliemann had brought back was taken to the Shonebeck palace near Breslau, and the Lebus palace.

The children who broke pots for sweets

The zoo and the Prussian State Bank were totally destroyed during the Second World War, taking with them the golden treasures. Only fragments of the finds remain, in other museums. Nothing remains of Lebus either. It was plundered and then pulled down at the end of the war. A scholar went to the palace just after the war and bribed children with sweets to bring her pieces of pottery that they could find. They were as business-minded as Schliemann. Instead of bringing her one whole pot, they smashed the vessels and received more sweets.

It is the custom at German weddings to smash pottery for luck. When the war was over the old pottery was thought to be a cheap way of wishing the bride and groom good luck without spending money, so more was lost this way.

The dream of the six-year-old boy is now almost entirely destroyed.

The golden potato field

It was 1868, and a boy had been sent out to an old fort not far from Ardagh, in County Limerick, which had been planted with potatoes. Potatoes were very important in Ireland, for in those days everyone depended on them for food and without them many would have died of hunger. Some potatoes seemed to be growing in between the roots of an old thorn bush, and the boy tried to dig these away to get at the vegetables. It was more difficult than he had imagined, for a stone slab was also tangled in the roots. He heaved it up. There at his feet was the glint of silver and gold, and the flash of colours.

What the boy had discovered was the finest treasure ever to come from Irish soil. It was a silver chalice, decorated with gold and coloured enamels, as well as rock crystal.

Alongside it were four beautiful large silver brooches, and a small bronze chalice. It is believed that the Ardagh Chalice (as it is called) was made around 700 AD and may have been hidden in the fort many centuries later, when religious troubles meant that the treasures stored in Irish monasteries were in danger of being destroyed.

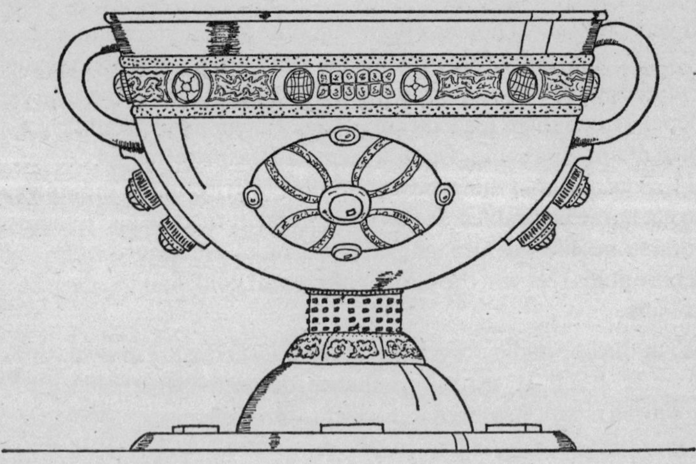

The Ardagh Chalice

The porpoise and the stone

One of the finest treasures ever unearthed in Britain was found in
1958 by a Shetland boy. He had heard that archaeologists were
digging up the old church on St Ninian's Isle, off the east coast of
the Shetland mainland, and as he was bored he decided he would go
and ask if they needed any help. They said they did, and set him to
work scraping the earth in the centre of the church. His scraping
laid bare a broken slab of sandstone, marked with a cross. The
archaeologists were excited, as this looked older than the church
itself. The boy raised the stone, and there, before his eyes, was a
hoard of 27 silver objects in a larchwood box. When he first saw
them they were grimy and discoloured, but after they were cleaned
they were seen to be superb works of art, made perhaps a century
after the Ardagh Chalice and buried here for fear that
they might be stolen by fierce Viking raiders.

There were silver bowls, brooches, sword chapes, a sword pommel
and mounts for its baldrick. There was also a silver bowl which had
been suspended from chains, and a spoon with a dog's head at the
end of the handle licking from the bowl. Each piece was richly
decorated, some with fantastic intertwining animals. And alongside
all these treasures was a mystery object. The jawbone of a porpoise.
Could it have been some magical charm ? Nobody knows or can
guess.

7 Pirate treasures and sunken treasures

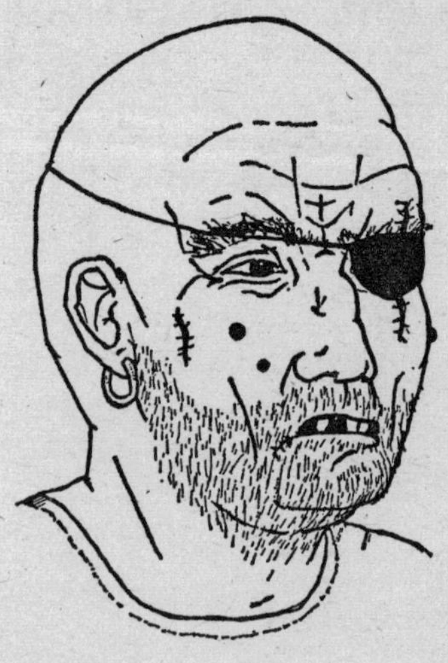

Pirates lived entirely in the hope of obtaining treasures for themselves. They were ruthless men who thought nothing of using violence to gain their ends; many exciting stories have been spun round their actions. Many pirates were heroes to their friends and their country. Sir Francis Drake was merely a pirate to the Spaniards, but a great hero in England. Pirates have existed as long as people have carried valuable goods by sea. The most successful sorties were usually when nations were at war – acts of piracy could be carried out on enemy ships that would have been illegal in peace-time. The Romans were menaced by pirates along the Mediterranean shores; the China seas were often sailed by pirates; and the most famous and feared sea raiders were the Vikings. Many hoards of gold and silver treasures that were buried for safety during Viking raids on France and Britain have been found.

The Spanish galleons that sailed to the West Indies or the Americas in the centuries after Christopher Columbus's voyage of discovery in 1492 were frequently set upon by pirates. The most famous flag in the world is the Jolly Roger.

Captain Kidd's treasure

The most famous pirates, like Long John Silver, are fictional. Of those who really did exist, Captain Kidd is the best known. He was probably born in Greenock, Scotland, in 1645. He rose in the world by trading with the West Indies, and by marrying a wealthy widow he became an important figure in New York society. For the first fifty years of his life he lived peaceably. There was little to suggest that he would deservedly meet his end on the gallows. In 1695, when he was well-settled in New York with his wife and children, he was officially employed to remove pirates who were menacing shipping. He was given permission to seize any French ship and to capture any pirates he came across.

The task was formidable. One of the most famous pirates at this time was Blackbeard. He was a horrible sight – he used to twist his long black hair with ribbons that dangled behind his ears. He also used to fix gunners' matches (foot-long fuses) behind his ears and light them so that smoke poured from his head.

Kidd eventually set sail with the blessing of the Admiralty and the Secretary of State, and with £6,000 to pay for the venture. His crew was an odd collection of sailors who became angry when there was little bounty during the first year. The pirates were too wily for them, and Kidd left friendly shipping alone. At last the crew became so angry at the lack of loot that there was a mutiny and Kidd only managed to stop the men by killing the gunner with a bucket.

After these difficulties Kidd seems to have changed his ideas and decided to attack all shipping. He was ready to fight French, English and pirates alike. The pirates in their base at Madagascar greeted him as though he were a friend.

After capturing several ships he used one of them, the *Quedagh Merchant*, as his own. Captain Kidd's successes as a pirate grew until at last he was arrested and his career was at an end. All the officials who had agreed to his venture in the first place were annoyed at his behaviour and there was little sympathy for him at his trial in London.

The treasure trick

During the trial Kidd offered the government a huge treasure which he said was worth £100,000. He said he would take them to where it lay hidden. The officials suspected that this was a trick and he was merely trying to gain his freedom by making up a story of treasure.

They refused to believe him and he was executed in 1701.
That should have been the end of the story.
Then, over the years, three maps turned up in old sea chests that
made people think that perhaps Captain Kidd had indeed known the
whereabouts of a splendid treasure. The last map came to light in
1934. Sadly there are very complicated instructions that cannot
be properly decoded. The island where the treasure lies is supposed
to be in the China Sea, not the area where Captain Kidd was most
active. It is thought that perhaps Kidd was not sure where the
treasure was. Perhaps he had merely gained possession of the map
and was intending to go out and seek it. We will probably never
know what the truth is, but if Kidd is to be believed, a vast treasure
is just waiting for someone to find it.

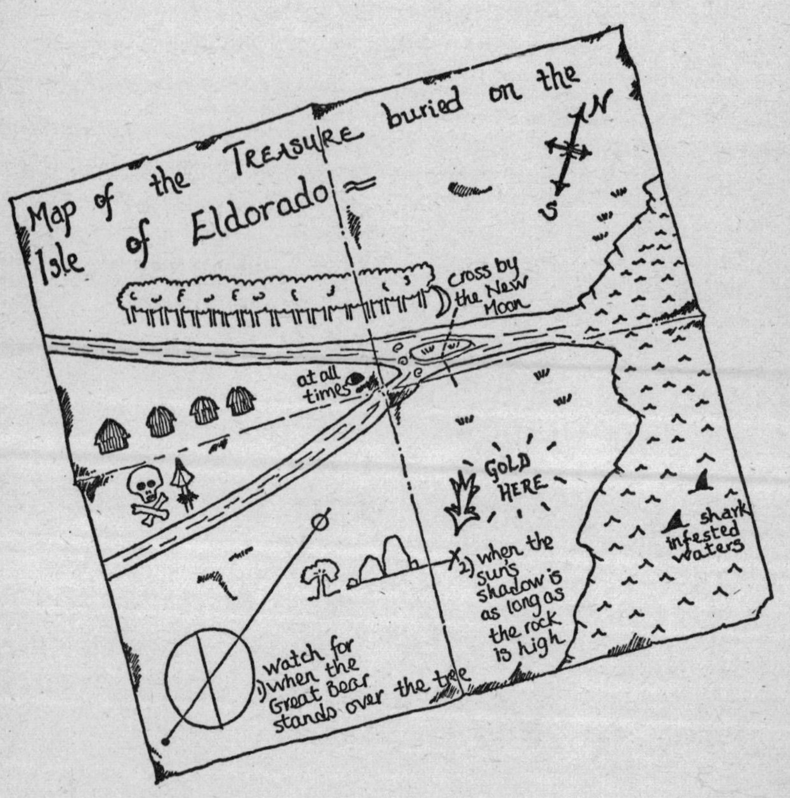

Henry Morgan's treasure

Henry Morgan is supposed to have been born in South Wales in
1635. He was either press-ganged into joining the crew of a ship
bound for the West Indies, or he joined up voluntarily. Once there,
he took part in the capture of Jamaica and by the time he was 31
he was second-in-command of the Port Royal privateers (ships with
government permission to attack enemy ships – really just legalized
pirates). At the captain's death he took over command. When
England made peace with Holland and France in 1667, he made his
first large capture. A brilliant attack on the town of Porto Bello
brought him a treasure of 250,000 coins known as pieces of eight and
other valuables.

Life was not easy for Morgan's Band – they went through many
hardships and at one point they had to boil their leather bags for
food.

At this time Panama was the richest port in the world, for it was the
centre of the silver and gold brought from the mountains. Morgan
took the town with much bloodshed but he was disappointed to
find little booty. The citizens were tortured, but the men received a
mere £10 each. It is possible that Morgan cheated his own men and
kept the gold of Panama for himself. He may have buried the gold
when he set sail for Jamaica later.

In 1672 Morgan was sent home to England for trial, but unlike
Captain Kidd he had public opinion on his side. The trial went well
for him and he was saved from the gallows. He returned to Jamaica,
not as a convicted criminal but as Lieutenant Governor. He finished
this life peaceably until an earthquake put part of Port Royal under
the sea in June 1692.

What happened to the treasure that Morgan is supposed to have
buried under the Caribbean Sea?

In 1965 Robert Marx was given permission to search under the sea
for treasure ships. He found two sunken wrecks in the first year of
diving, and many objects. One was a chest which bore the crest of the
Spanish king. Inside was a treasure worthy of any pirate: coins that
had been minted only a short while before they were lost. It is
possible that this was part of the treasure that Henry Morgan is
supposed to have lost three centuries ago.

Sunken treasures

Underwater treasures, like that in the Caribbean that might have been lost by Morgan, are often as exciting to find as they were to acquire in the first place. Until fairly recently it has been impossible to recover treasures from deep water – specialist diving equipment is needed. On the other hand when a ship was wrecked near habitation the locals rarely left the treasures without at least trying to recover them. Many a promising treasure hunt has ended in disappointment because someone else had been there before.

The first attempts to recover treasures were made surprisingly early, considering the difficulties. King John lost a great treasure in the Wash, and monks later tried to salvage it. They had no success. One eighteenth-century diver became known as *Jacob the Diver* because of his adventures. He used to dive to the remarkable depth of six or ten fathoms. Not surprisingly he recorded that his ears bled and that he was very uncomfortable.

The waters around the Isles of Scilly have been a good searching ground for treasure hunters. Many wrecks went down in these treacherous waters. Unfortunately the amount of equipment and capital need is often more than the price of the treasures discovered. Many have lost small fortunes trying to find large ones.

Many of the ships that have been found under the sea have contained treasures of different sorts. Very few have been found with chests or holds containing gold, jewels or silver. The most valuable cargoes are treasures of a different kind – these days even things that might seem to be boring, worthless pieces of pottery or ironwork can be auctioned for very large sums. These ships are not the sort of treasures we are talking about in this book, though many have been very exciting to find and to excavate. Indeed, so valuable are the finds in some cases that modern 'pirates' often harass the divers who have been given a licence to make searches. Some divers have even had to risk their lives, not from sharks, lack of oxygen, storms, or the other dangers generally met with by deep-sea divers, but from ruthless treasure seekers who are sometimes prepared to use shark spears or guns to take the sunken loot.

The searching of wrecks is a very specialist operation – often the very factors that caused the ships to founder in the first place will work against the divers. The Shetlands, the Scillies and other hazardous areas have wrecked many ships.

One treasure ship – *Die Liefde*, a Dutch East Indiaman – was wrecked off the Outer Skerries in Shetland in October 1711. All the crew of 300 were lost except one man. The cargo of 227,000 guilders was a valuable treasure but when modern divers searched they discovered

that nearly all the money had already been taken ; no doubt over the years there were large numbers of people willing to risk their lives to reach the shining coins.

Many of the stories of wrecks feature treasures. Two Viking warships were returning to Norway in 1151 after a successful plundering trip to Europe, when they went down off the Shetlands. Legend reports that there was much treasure aboard, which is probably true since the Vikings were skilled raiders and much feared. The ships have not been found yet, however, and the treasure lies sunken.

A more famous and more modern ship to go down with a vast fortune aboard is the *Lusitania*. It is known that when the ship was torpedoed by a German U-boat in 1915, she sank 11 miles (17·69 km) south-east of the Head of Kinsale. Over 11,000 passengers drowned, and gold, silver and diamonds aboard worth at least £500,000 were lost. There have been unsuccessful efforts to retrieve this treasure.

Other hunts have been more successful. The *Hollandia* was a ship wrecked on her maiden voyage in 1743. The captain had in his possession 129,700 guilders, a very large sum. Unfortunately for the 276 crew and soldiers and the 30 passengers, this Dutch ship sank off the Scillies. Efforts were made to salvage her but without success. Then on 16 September 1971 divers specializing in searching for wrecks came across the cannon and anchors of the ship. The head of the exploration was Rex Cowan. He had already been granted a licence to explore for lost Dutch ships, but unfortunately the ship lay outside the area covered by the permission. If he could get a licence, 25 per cent of the valuables on board the *Hollandia* which belonged to Holland would be his.

A race began between the finders and many others who, like pirates of old, hovered round, trying to find the treasure to take it illegally for themselves. The location was kept a secret but finally the secret leaked out.

Even when permission was obtained, the operation was difficult. Each diver could stay under water for a mere 30 minutes at a time, and had to keep returning for rest periods. The working day was not long. But the efforts were worth it. The *Hollandia* had been virtually untouched over the years. She lay at the bottom of the sea in exactly the position in which she had sunk. The timbers and other flimsy objects had perished, but rings and guns, pewter plate, silver and coins were all there to be found. There were thousands and thousands of silver cobs and reales (coins). The silver coins had probably been originally brought from Peru.

The value of the find was a real treasure – even a fine bronze military mortar (a type of gun) was auctioned for £2,500.

8 How to find treasure

There is no reason why you should not find treasure yourself, as long as you are careful to follow a few simple rules. Treasure hunting can be completely free and great fun – even if you do not discover a great treasure you will certainly find *something* of interest. You may find that your searches lead to new hobbies – gem-stone polishing or jewellery making, archaeology or geology. You may even be inspired to take up new sports – diving, climbing or pot-holing, though for these you *must* have expert teachers and not try to do it yourself.

It is very important to keep treasure hunting in proportion. It is

not worth risking everything for treasure. Many of the most exciting treasure hunts were carried out by men who were cruel, ruthless, and hard, with nothing to lose but their own lives. On the other hand, a very large amount of treasure has been found quite safely by chance. In many ways it is more difficult to know *when* you have found treasure than it is to find it in the first place.

The rules you should observe are for your own safety and for that of others. They will also ensure that you will be able to keep the treasure you find and that you do not accidentally annoy or anger other people. They are listed in brief below with fuller explanations following. Read them all in detail before treasure hunting.

Summary of the rules for young treasure hunters

1 Safety first.
2 Do not disturb ancient sites; do not dig deeply.
3 Ask permission to search.
4 Do not leave a mess, and pick up any litter.
5 Report finds of gold or silver to the local museum.
6 Follow the country code.
7 Keep records.

Safety first

Use your common sense to decide where it is safe to search. *Do not* search in rivers or under the sea (even with a snorkel). *Do not* look in pot-holes, old mines, caves or along cliffs or screes (the piles of stones at the foot of hills or mountains). All these places need special skills to explore. It is consoling to note that there are plenty of treasures to be found in safe places – smugglers' caves, for instance, might seem exciting places to search, but they are probably dangerous and someone will almost certainly have been there before you and taken any treasure long ago. Muddy banks and river flats have been a favourite hunting place for treasure seekers. Sadly, the holes that have been dug have not always been filled in again and they fill up with water. The holes then look exactly the same as the firm mud and many accidents have occurred. It is best to leave mud flats or rivers alone. Dumps are not good places to search because of the dangers – children have been killed on bottle dumps, for instance. Take no chances and always search, wherever you may be, with at least one friend.

Pot-holing, mining or investigating wells needs specialized skills, money and many skilled helpers and equipment.

There is, too, the possibility that you might find live ammunition – cartridges or even mines. Never touch anything suspicious. Make a note of the exact spot where you found the object and tell the police at once. If you follow the rule below about not digging deeply you should not get into such difficulties.

Ancient sites

Archaeologists and historians have often been angered by treasure
hunters in the past. This is because the hunters have sometimes
behaved badly, digging up ancient sites and destroying evidence. It
is very difficult to interpret the changes in the soil that are all we
have to tell us what went on in the past, and large holes dug without
the help of expert archaeologists can make the task impossible.
People have often destroyed valuable information without realizing
what they were doing.

You will not annoy archaeologists, however, if you *do not dig below
the topsoil*. This is the part of the soil in which the little flowers
grow and small animals burrow. It is softer than the soil below and
often of a different colour. It has already been churned up so much
that archaeologists cannot make use of it. The topsoil can be from
about three feet (just under a metre) to only an inch or two (a
couple of centimetres) deep. As a general rule if you do not dig
below about six inches (15 cm) you will have no trouble. If you learn
to recognize when the topsoil ends you will be able to dig deeper in
some places. If the soil becomes a different colour or is more
compacted as you dig down, stop because you will probably have
dug through the topsoil and might be destroying archaeological
evidence. If you find a treasure that is embedded in deeper soil, the
best thing to do would be to call in an archaeologist to help you to
remove it. However, this might not be very practical and there is
always the danger that someone else might dig up your treasure while
you were away getting help. In this case try to remove the treasure
with as little mess as possible. Do not dig a huge hole all around it –
just ease it out and then inform the experts. This is not very likely
to happen, however, since there are plenty of treasures for you to
find that are in the topsoil – many of the most splendid have been
found in this part of the soil.

It is illegal to dig on an ancient site that is protected by the state.
Sometimes there is a notice on the site but in most cases there is
not. To be on the safe side do not dig if a place is marked on the
Ordnance Survey map as an ancient site – it might be called stones,
castle, villa, cemetery or several other names. However, some in
state care are not marked.

Permission

It is very important to have the permission of the owner of the land you want to search for treasure. You must say you are looking for treasure – if you had permission to fish, for instance, and accidentally found treasure, your find would belong to the landowner. Make sure the person you ask is the landowner and not just the tenant. If a public body owns the land you should still ask – this might take a bit longer but is worth it to be able to keep your treasures. Treasure belongs to the landowner unless he or she has given permission to a hunter to hunt.

Do not leave a mess

Landowners will not be pleased if you leave a mess. Fill in any holes you make or you might not be allowed back again. This would be sad if you found real treasure and wanted to return for more. Pick up and take home any cans, foil or bottle tops and never just throw them away. If you use a metal detector, these will give a positive reaction and can be very disappointing finds! By taking them away you can be of service to the countryside as well as helpful to other treasure hunters.

Reporting finds

Anything made of gold or silver must be reported to the local museum since it might be Treasure Trove. The laws about this differ slightly in each country, but basically if the gold or silver found (in England) has been buried for ever and the owner had no intention of returning for it the finder will own the find (provided he had permission to search). This is the case if the gold or silver were found in a grave, for instance.

However, if the original owner can be proved to have wanted to return for his treasure, the find will belong to the Crown and will be declared treasure trove. In this case the full market value of the find will be paid to the finder. It is thus very important to report any find as soon as you find out it is made of gold or silver: if you tried to hide your find you would not be given a reward.

The country code

This means shutting all gates behind you, not disturbing any sheep, cattle or other animals, not leaving litter or damaging crops in any way. In fact, it means leaving the countryside exactly as you found it without upsetting either people or animals.

Keeping records

It is best to keep a record of your finds in a notebook. You should note where you found your treasure and when, and what it looks like.

When you find treasure of any kind you should give it a number even if you are not sure if it is valuable. Write the number on a luggage label and tie it firmly to the find. Then put the label and the find in a paper bag or polythene bag and write the same number on this. Put the number in your notebook along with the other information and you will always have all the information readily available when you need it. If you do not realize what a treasure you have found until much later you will still be able to say where you found it. This is important because if it is of great interest archaeologists might want to dig at the find-spot to discover more information about the find if possible. This would put up the value of your find. You may also wish to go back and find more treasures if one place is proving particularly fruitful.

DATE	TREASURE	LOCATION
3:3:78	Twisted metal about 3 feet long. Silver?	In Eastern corner of field next to Post Office in village of Snodbury. Sticking out of furrow.
9:3:78	Crock of gold coins	Corner of filled-in building site at Grange Street, Birmingpool. Lying on the ground at the end of a rainbow.

If you are very lucky your record book might look something like this

Where to search

Almost anywhere that is safe is a good place to search for treasures,
though some places are better than others and you can only learn
from experience where these may be. Start with your own garden if
you have one (even a window box can have some sort of treasures,
as long as it was filled from a garden and not from compost bought
in a shop). The nearest piece of wasteland, hedgerow or park, lane,
field or beach or open ground near trees in large towns, will almost
certainly have something for you to find. With a bit of luck, there is
no reason why you should not find watches, ancient swords, gold
necklaces or coins in any of these places.

How to know when you have found treasure

This is the most difficult part of treasure hunting. The problem is
not made easier by the fact that there are many different kinds of
treasure. These days, almost anything old has a value in money –
old bottles, pottery, glass, clay tobacco pipes as well as more obvious
things like gold or silver. Archaeological treasures consist of
everything that has ever been made! These are special kinds of
treasure and do not usually have much value in money terms. They
need to be treated with care and the *Young Archaeologist's Handbook*
(Piccolo 1976, Severn House 1977) by Lloyd and Jennifer Laing
will tell you nearly all you need to know about finding them.
If you decide you are only interested in treasures like gold or silver
it can still be difficult to know when you have hit the jackpot. Gold
does not rust but it can look very dull and dirty after years in the
soil. Silver tarnishes very quickly and after a long time might look
brown or purplish. Coins might seem easy to recognize, but the
oldest coins are often ugly lumps of metal without letters on them.
Yet they can be very valuable. The best advice is to start looking and
when you have found an object, take it along to your local museum
and see if you can see anything like it. If it seems likely to be of
interest or value ask the museum staff to help. Other experts to ask
might be the local archaeologist if there is one, the local university
department of archaeology, the local library, or a school's museum
officer.

If you find something of value in your attic or a junk store you can
either find out from a museum what it is, or look it up in a library
book on antiques. It is not likely to be more than a couple of

hundred years old at the most, so you will have some idea where to start. Again, if it seems likely to be of value, take it along to your local museum and get their advice.

Common treasures you might find

Gold coins – look out for small discs with lettering or pictures or just bumps on them. Rings, bracelets, chains, watches are common and almost any inlays – anything from teeth to furniture can be decorated with gold which can work loose and be lost. Look out for hallmarks which are signs put on gold objects by the maker. Libraries usually have books on hallmarks which will help you identify any gold.

Silver cutlery is very common – often brown or purple in colour, it will clean up well. It can be solid silver or just plated and may have a hallmark. The variety of silver objects you might find is as varied as those in gold. Coins are often made of silver.

Precious stones These will probably be in good condition when you find them and may have been lost from jewellery. Some can be carved like cameos or they may still be in their settings.

Archaeological treasures These are very varied, from glass, pottery, iron to ivory or bone – almost anything, in fact. They are usually broken and are rarely worth money.

Aids to treasure hunting

Sifting The cheapest method of looking for treasure is by sifting through the soil. For this you need little or no equipment. A small trowel is really all you might need, with a container for finds and some bags and labels and a pen for marking the finds (see p. 89). It is probably not worth using a fine sieve at first, though this is probably the only way you will find very small objects such as gemstones that have been lost. You are more likely to find larger objects, and it would be more exciting to start off finding things quickly. Start on whatever piece of open ground you have chosen and look in the topsoil. It is best to start at one end and move across it slowly so you do not miss anything. If you find things (broken pottery for instance) that you do not want, leave them where they are. Choose parts of gardens where you will not disturb bulbs or flowers!

Dowsing Some people have the ability to dowse for water, or for
metal. To find out whether you have this ability is important for a
treasure hunter, since it can save you time and effort in searching.
The idea is that you carry a hazel stick over the ground and when
you reach a piece of metal (or water, or whatever it is that you are
sensitive to) buried underground, the stick will start to twitch. This
sounds impossible but really does work for some people. The stick
must be the right kind, however. To make a dowsing stick take a
hazel stick shaped like a Y. Peel off the bark and dry the stick out.
Then sharpen the point. Hold it either with the point towards
you or away from you (grasping the two smaller points of the Y with
your hands). Holding it flat (parallel to the ground) slowly walk up
and down the area you want to search. The rod will move upwards
or downwards when you pass over whatever you are able to find.
Test whether you have this ability before you start hunting or you
will waste your time. Put a piece of metal under the ground (or get
someone else to if you think you might make the stick twitch yourself
if you know where the metal is hidden) and then pass over it with
the stick. Do the same with water – pass over a place where you
know there is a drain and see if the stick twitches.

Metal detectors These are expensive to buy but can be useful in
finding treasures. They will certainly help you find anything made of
metal. Sadly this includes silver foil and old tin cans, so they can be
rather disappointing if you keep hitting the jack-pot only to find
that the 'treasure' is rubbish. At the same time they can lead to
spectacular finds and sometimes can lead to the discovery of
important archaeological sites. One lady in 1977 found silver chalices
and candleholders with her metal detector the first time she used it.
She found a second hoard of silver a short distance away. It turned
out that it was loot from a robbery at a nearby house and had been
hidden away till the thieves thought it was safe to return. Some
thieves have died before they could return. Other hoards were put
in the ground before banks were invented.

Gem hunting Gems of all kinds can be found. You will need
nothing more costly than a small hammer and chisel, a penknife
and a magnifying glass, as well as a container for your finds. A book
on gems and a *pair of goggles* to prevent splinters of rock from
damaging your eyes are both essential. Ask permission to search, as
in all treasure hunting, if the land does not belong to you.

In Britain diamonds have been found as well as less rare stones;
topaz, garnets, opals and quartz. This can be a very rewarding
hobby.

Beachcombing This is probably the most enjoyable way for the
young treasure hunter to find treasures. It is absolutely safe and
very productive. People have been losing things in the sea for years,
and the sea tends to wash things up on the shore. People changing
into swimming costumes or fumbling in their pockets to pay for
ice-creams lose money and small objects like watches all the time.
The best places to look are near ice-cream, candy floss and hamburger
stalls on sandy beaches. All you need is time and patience. A metal
detector can be useful for this since it saves time but it will also
react to tin cans and it might be just as easy to use a bucket and spade
to sift the sand. The advantage of beachcombing is that you will
almost certainly recognize at once the treasures you find since they
will probably be modern. Old coins can be impossible to recognize
but a 10p piece can not only be recognized but can be spent on the
spot without having to see experts and valuers. The only warnings
to heed are:

1 Look out for slippery rock pools and stick to safe sandy beaches.
2 Do make sure the things you find really are lost and that the owner
is not looking for them too! It would be stealing if you 'found'
things people had merely left behind when going off for a swim.

If in doubt, if you find something of value, you should take it to
the police station. If the object is not claimed within two months
you can claim it back yourself.

Lloyd and Jennifer Laing
The Young Archaeologist's Handbook 40p

Archaeology? Why not have a go?

This is an unusual book which shows you how to make a 'find' and
document it, how to plan an expedition, how to use the museums,
and what to look out for in town and in the countryside.

Anthony Greenbank
Survival for Young People 60p

Anyone, any time, can be faced with an emergency, indoors or out. If
a fire traps you in a room, someone is drowning or you are lost in
unknown territory, would you know what to do? Read this book and
you will be prepared for most of them.

Deborah Manley and Pamela Cotterill
Maps and Map Games 45p

If you are interested in maps this is the book for you. It tells you
everything you need to know about maps – how to use them, draw
them, follow them, and how to orienteer. And it's packed with line
drawings and diagrams which clearly explain the text.

Deborah Manley
Piccolo All the Year Round Book 50p

This is a superb 'year book' to dip into throughout the twelve months.
Every month contains a wealth of ideas for things to make and do, facts
about weather and history, famous birthdays, seasonal poems and
much, much more.

LaVada Weir
Skateboards and Skateboarding 50p

Illustrated with drawings and photographs

From America . . . the complete handbook and beginner's guide.
From how to choose and look after your skateboard and how to build
one, to advanced skateboarding manoeuvres like three-sixties and the
slalom – all the advice you need for skilful, sensible and, above all, safe
skateboarding.

Richard Ballantine
The Piccolo Bicycle Book 60p

Everything you need to know about the bicycle from how to choose
one, and how to learn to ride it, to how to maintain it in good order.
The author also tells the reader about the Highway Code, road
safety, cycling clubs and holiday associations.

Elizabeth Hogarth
Wigwams, Igloos and Bungalows 45p

A survey of the different types of buildings people live in all over the
world, with plenty of funny drawings of them.

Geoffrey Trease
Days to Remember 60p

For every month of the year, here are pages of historical anniversaries
from almost a thousand years of history – events of the past, great and
small, from Alfred the Great and the Danes to the true story of Dick
Whittington.

Richard Garrett
Narrow Squeaks 50p

Fascinating, hair-raising stories of people who, against all odds,
escaped disaster . . . The man who jumped from an aeroplane $3\frac{1}{2}$ miles
up in the air – and survived . . . The young girl who survived *ten days*
of lonely danger in the Peruvian jungle . . . Whether it's luck, faith or
determination, nobody knows. This is a book of true mysteries – or
miracles!

Great Sea Mysteries 50p

A collection of fascinating stories of great oceans and strange ships,
master-spies and mutineers, sabotage and the supernatural, the
heroism of young Grace Darling, and the never-ending mystery of the
Mary Celeste . . .

Hoaxes and Swindles 50p

From the remarkable affair of the Abyssinian princess to the artist
whose masterpiece fooled a continent . . . from a prehistoric skull to
famous hoaxes on radio and TV . . . here is a fascinating collection of
true stories from many countries.